The Elements of
INTERNATIONAL
ENGLISH
Style

The Elements of
INTERNATIONAL
ENGLISH
Style

A GUIDE TO WRITING
CORRESPONDENCE, REPORTS,
TECHNICAL DOCUMENTS,
and INTERNET PAGES
FOR A GLOBAL AUDIENCE

EDMOND H. WEISS

M.E.Sharpe
Armonk, New York
London, England

All brand names and product names used in this book are trade names,
services marks, trademarks, or registered trademarks of their respective owners,
and have been appropriately capitalized. M.E. Sharpe, Inc., is not
associated with any product or vendor mentioned in this book.

Library of Congress Cataloging-in-Publication Data

Weiss, Edmond H.
    The elements of international English style : a guide to writing English correspon-
dence, reports, technical documents, and internet pages for a global audience / by Edmond
H. Weiss.
        p. cm.
    Includes bibliographical references and index.
    ISBN 0-7656-1571-1 (hardcover : alk. paper)
    1. English language—Style—Handbooks, manuscripts, etc. 2. Communication,
International—Handbooks, manuals, etc. 3. English language—Textbooks for foreign
speakers. 4. Web sites—Design—Handbooks, manuals, etc. 5. Technical writing—
Handbooks, manuals, etc. 6. Report writing—Handbooks, manuals, etc. 7. Letter
writing—Handbooks, manuals, etc. I. Title.

PE1421.W39 2005
808′.042—dc22   2004021680

Printed in the United States of America

The paper used in this publication meets the minimum requirements of
American National Standard for Information Sciences
Permanence of Paper for Printed Library Materials,
ANSI Z 39.48-1984.

BM (c)   10   9   8   7   6   5   4   3   2   1

For My Daughter, Meredith

*An appropriate style will adapt itself
to the emotions of the hearers . . .*
—Aristotle

*Whether you are developing information for
non-native speakers of English or information that
a vendor is going to translate, you must write
in an international style that transcends culture.*
—Marlana Coe

Contents

Preface

Several years ago, a client (one of the world's largest corporations) approached me with a problem. According to the firm's market research, more than half the people visiting the company's website were reading English as their second language—and the proportion was increasing daily. Given this trend, the client asked, should the company rethink its editorial policies, develop new standards for writers (whom they called "content providers"), perhaps even develop an alternative version of the website for persons with less than fluent English?

After several discussions, we realized that most of the conflicting alternatives involved a clash between two principles: *globalization*, producing a one-size-fits-all solution for a diverse world of English speakers, versus *localization*, adapting and modifying this universal model for particular readers, in particular locales. The first principle proposes, for example, the elimination of nearly all figurative language (no "ballpark estimates" or "advertising blitzes"); the second recommends the use of English figures and idioms that resemble those peculiar to the first language of the reader ("one may access the account by the Internet" for German speakers of English, for example).

To some extent, everyone engaged in international business or the international exchange of ideas (business, government, science, education) confronts these controversies repeatedly. For example, in sending a letter to confirm your European hotel arrangements, should you write in an especially clear, lean, "bullet" style, even though some cultures regard the use of bullets as a sign of poor education? In preparing an English report for a Chinese reader, should you put a hyphen in the word "mis-led," knowing that such a hyphen, helpful as it might be to the reader, is incorrect punctuation?

English is the first language of about 400 million people (*E1s*). But there are more than another billion people who speak it either as a second language (*E2s*), usually in their business or profession, or as a foreign language (*E3s*), speaking or reading only rarely, as needed. As difficult as it is to communicate clear, unambiguous information to E1s, it is even more difficult to communicate with E2s, who read and evaluate an increasingly larger proportion of our business and technical documents.

The labels E1, E2, and E3 used above are adaptations of David Crystal's L1, L2, and L3 in *English as a Global Language* (Cambridge University Press, 1997) and refer generally to those who speak a particular tongue as their first, second, or foreign language. In my adaptation, E2 speaks English as a second language; M2 speaks Mandarin Chinese as a second language. Although this system may sometimes appear insensitive and mechanistic, it is preferable to such long-winded expressions as "those who speak English as a second language" and to such culturally charged terms as *native* or *mother-tongue.*

All communication risks misunderstanding, and communication between E1s and E2s simply increases those risks. As this book explains, sometimes the best way to contain the risk is to write in an unusually readable style—using short words, short sentences, and elementary verb forms, and eliminating idioms such as *stone's throw* and expressions with many meanings, such as *have been detained.*

Sometimes, however, this first set of tactics—which are common to much good business and technical writing—needs to be modified to suit E2. Familiar, clear words, including *make, set, fix,* or *hold,* can have too many context-dependent meanings and might better be replaced with longer words that have fewer meanings: *construct, define, repair,* or *conclude,* for example. Everyday phrasal verbs, notably *check out,* might be replaced with *investigate* or *leave,* depending on what is intended.

This book presents both kinds of tactics—advice and examples— on how to turn a first draft by an E1 writer into a draft more suitable for E2 readers. Its main audiences are

- Business students, graduate and undergraduate, especially those concerned with international business who find that their texts do not adequately address the problems of International English,
- Communication students, especially those preparing for careers in business and technical writing/editing,
- Trainers and seminar leaders, especially those who organize and facilitate workshops and short courses on international and intercultural communication,
- Business professionals, especially those who have become aware of the difficulties and frustrations of using English as a global language of commerce, and
- Writers and editors (business and technical) whose job is to revise E1's drafts and prepare them for an international readership.

Although E2s who also write English as their second language will get many good ideas from this text, it is mainly intended for E1s. In many ways, the more facile and comfortable one is in writing English, the more prone one is to making the many errors explained here. For example, whether to start an International English sentence with *although* is only an issue for writers who start sentences with *although*. (Not everyone does.)

International business communication is filled with small tactical problems and must resolve many serious ethical, economic, and philosophical questions as well. For example: How much should the sender of a message be expected to adapt to the limitations of the receiver? Is it ever ethical for an honorable person to be ambiguous, even when that person is writing to people who prefer ambiguity? Will the Internet eventually familiarize all English speakers with American figures of speech? Is it necessary to be gender-sensitive in International English, when most of the first languages spoken by E2s have a nonpolitical view of gender in language? What should companies do if they plan to use machine translation of their documents and web pages?

The research for this book began as a rather disorganized, continually growing list of high-level strategic questions about communication and culture, interspersed with tiny, particular questions about how to spell things and where to use hyphens. Over the years I have tried to tame this disorder with the simple structure contained in this book. After setting the context and defining the terms of International English Style, I organize the material into these categories:

- Principles of Simplicity, that is, how to choose the right words and phrases for an E2 document.
- Principles of Clarity, that is, how to reduce the chances that passages and sentences will mislead or befuddle the E2 reader.
- Reducing Burdens, that is, decreasing the effort and stress associated with a passage or document, increasing the chances the E2 will understand it correctly.
- Writing for Translation, that is, focusing the advice so far in ways that support and simplify the work of translators—human or machine.
- Principles of Correspondence, that is, the special issues of style and manner associated with formal letters, on the one hand, and less formal e-mail, on the other.
- Principles of Cultural Adaptation, that is, broader, contextual concerns about the barriers between cultures and the ethical ambiguities in intercultural exchanges.
- Appendixes with projects for teachers, students, and workshop leaders.

Except for the Appendixes, each chapter concludes with discussion questions related to the topic of the chapter. Although the link between topic and question may not initially be apparent, all the questions are indeed germane and productive. In every case, the question is meant to stimulate a discussion that will lead either to the clear conclusions of the previous chapter or, in a few cases, to an important irresolvable controversy. So, the chapter on clarity asks: *Have you ever lost time or money trying to follow unclear instructions?* This query should underscore the economic value of editing and revising, which is the main reason for making business documents clearer. In contrast, a question at the end of the chapter on burdens asks students about the different levels of difficulty in the texts they use and their effect on them. This question should lead to a provocative argument about the responsibilities of authors and publishers to their readers, with some discussants noting that many successful and respected sources feel no obligation to reduce the burden on their readers at all.

As a final note, the reader should be aware that most of *The Elements of International Style* is not written in International English Style, even though it is laced with examples and illustrations. For example, "laced with" would be the wrong choice for an E2 reader. Although it is relatively easy and straightforward to use this style to present certain long documents such as service manuals or product specifications, it is quite another thing to write a hundred pages of concepts, anecdotes, and insights without some wordplay, figurative language, and more than an occasional complex sentence. When International English documents are well prepared, they are clear, efficient, reliable, readable, and translatable; for these reasons, they are also rather dull and colorless.

The objective of this book is not only to provide the hard facts (replacement tables, revised passages, rules of usage and punctuation), but also to stimulate thought and provoke controversy. A lifetime of teaching professional people to write and speak has taught me that technique is never enough; what all the best communicators have in common is imagination—a trait that this book is meant to stimulate.

Acknowledgments

The idea for this project began during an idyllic two weeks at the East-West Center in Honolulu; I thank the Fordham Business School, particularly Ernest Scalberg, for making the trip possible. The research for this book also grew partly from my training and consulting engagements with Microsoft Corporation; I thank especially Barbara Roll and Lesley Link for their ideas and encouragement. Thanks also to Frank Taylor, currently President of the Israeli Chapter of the *Society for Technical Communication,* as well as Paula Berger and Lynne Harris of the sorely missed *Solutions* training company, and Nurel Beylerian of BOMAR Marketing, all of whom provided opportunities to test and refine this material in professional seminars. Finally, I owe a debt to Stan Wakefield for finding this project a publisher, as well as to my editor, Niels Aaboe, for bringing it to fruition.

The Elements of
INTERNATIONAL
ENGLISH
Style

1

The Language of Global Business Is International English

Business and technical documents intended for those who read English as their second language must be unusually simple, unambiguous, and literal. Ideally, they should be edited for ease of translation. They must also be free of cultural irritants and distractions. Every native speaker of English (E1) must learn to edit and revise documents meant for international readers.

A Riddle

Here's a riddle heard on a business trip to the Middle East:

Question: If a person who speaks many languages is called multilingual and a person who speaks two languages is called bilingual, what is a person called who speaks only one language?

Answer: An American.

In the 1960s, there was much talk about "Ugly Americans"—travelers from the United States who regarded the cultures, politics, and civilizations of other countries as backwards and inferior. Characteristically, ugly Americans spoke only English (the American version), and, moreover, they expected that, if they spoke loudly and slowly enough, everyone in the world would understand them.

Today, such travelers, even if they are not more enlightened, have an easier time of it. Nearly one-fourth of the people on Earth speak English well enough to perform everyday tasks and share the ideas that occur in normal conversation. But most of that group, more than a billion people, speak English as their *second* language, not their first. Although many people throughout the globe lament the rapid spread of English, complaining that it has displaced and obviated other languages, English has gained currency mainly as a second language, not a first. No demographic projection in any study shows that English is becoming the first language of significantly more people. In fact, the British organization charged with estimating the future of the English language predicts the opposite: that the proportion of native speakers of English (referred to in this text as E1s) in the world will continue to decline in this century and may even be overtaken in its second position by Hindi/Urdu. Indeed, in the United States, English is already losing ground to Spanish (Gradol, 2000).

Those of us who are E1s and who study the international uses of English do not expect it to replace any major language, except, perhaps, for certain specific international uses such as scientific journals. On the contrary, the purpose of this text is to remind those with the best grasp of English, who acquired that ability without the ardors of learning a second language, that they have an added responsibility when they communicate with those who read English as their second language (E2s). Nor does this text suggest that Americans—or anyone else—should be smug about knowing only English. Living well in the twenty-first century—being a good citizen and an effective professional—virtually requires us to learn at least one other language, at least well enough to make friends when we travel. Such knowledge will improve our ability to write and speak in an *International English Style*.

What Is *International English Style?*

Language researchers estimate that English is the most widely spoken language in the world. The current estimate is that about 1.5 billion people speak English well enough to use the language for business or education. Less than a third of these, however, speak English as their first language (E1); there are only about 400 million E1s in the world, and about half of them are in one country: the United States of America.

There are also about 1.5 billion speakers of Mandarin Chinese. The main difference, however, is that about two-thirds of them speak Chinese as their first language (M1) and only a third as a second language (M2).

Furthermore, for various demographic reasons, the number of E1s is declining, if not absolutely then as a proportion of the world's population, whereas the number of E2s is growing. That is, the typical writer/reader of English is increasingly someone who has learned it as a second language. It is projected that by the middle of the twenty-first century, most of the countries that have an official second language will have selected English as that language. Thus, in those countries that publish official documents in two languages, the second will probably be English; in those countries that require children to learn a foreign language, that language will be English; and in those countries that demand second-language competence as a condition of employment in the government or civil service, English will usually be that language. (One Chinese leader has expressed the goal that *all* Chinese people should learn English.)

Currently, hundreds of thousands (perhaps millions) of school children are enrolled in compulsory or strongly recommended English courses throughout the world. These students know that not only their academic careers but their ultimate earning power will be shaped to some extent by how well they can conjugate the exasperating English verb *to lay* or pronounce correctly the illogically spelled *says*. One can also suspect that most of these students are pursuing the language reluctantly, especially in those countries where English is associated with colonialism or with controversial American foreign policy or transnational corporations.

When David Crystal calls English a "global language," he is talking about its widespread study and use by nonnative speakers: E2s. What makes English a global language is the *way* it is used: to support international commerce, to unify communities with diverse languages, and to provide a *lingua franca*, a universal language, much as Latin became in the Middle Ages and French until the early twentieth century.

This gradual displacement of Latin and then French with English as the language of international diplomacy in the West (U.S. passports are still in English AND French) is neither the result of some organized campaign by English speakers nor the decree of some international standards organization. No rule requires that three-fourths of the world's scientific papers are to be published in English. No world body, for example, coerced the Association Europeene de Constructeurs de Materiel

Aerospatial (AECMA), a Belgian organization, to make English the official language of the world aircraft industry. Rather, English emerged as a global language in the twentieth Century through the combined effect of American economic and military power. (In contrast, British influence was in sharp decline in the last century.)

By International English Style, I mean an approach to English that reflects an appreciation of its global uses and sensitivity to the needs of the E2 reader. Of course, not all E2s require special treatment. People with an aptitude for languages can master two or three of them, writing and speaking not only competently but beautifully in all. Some of the finest prose in English is the work of E2s, including some by writers who did not begin the study of the language until they were adults.

For the most part, however, International English will be read not by the linguistically gifted but, rather, by those tens of millions of ordinary folks who were coerced by school systems or compelled by economic necessity to learn this quirky tongue with its exotic spelling, esoteric rules of word order, and huge, synonym-filled vocabulary. Most of them, moreover, will be using an alphabet different from their own—always an immensely difficult task—and perhaps even a separate keyboard for their word processor. In addition, a good many may even resent the fact that America's economic or military might has forced them to set aside their own language and to sacrifice their own comfort and fluency.

Imagine, for instance, how the French feel about the use of English in European websites or how they regard Algeria's decision to make English, not French, its official second language. France is one of the few countries still policing its business communications to keep out incipient English words. Or think of a billion Indians, and their tense history with Britain, who are obliged to use English to bridge the language gaps within their linguistically diverse country or as a way to secure those controversial "outsourced" American jobs. Empathize for a moment with those who see English as a linguistic juggernaut, driving minor languages out of existence and devaluing fluency in any other tongue.

An awareness of these political and cultural frustrations is also a part of International English Style, along with the more technical concern for using words and sentences in ways that are most likely to be understood and translated correctly. In effect, whenever we write for a large E2 audience, we are writing for translation. The purpose of this text, therefore, is to offer advice to everyone who writes for E2 readers: people who read English as their second language, typically as part of their work or education.

Generally, the following pages contain lists of tactics and tips that will help the reader learn how to handle word choice, punctuation, or verb forms. These tactics follow from two broad communication precepts of International English Style:

- First, reduce the burden on the E2 reader in every way possible, but without condescending or "writing down."
- Second, write for translation, that is, for a reader who might consult a bilingual dictionary.

Nearly all good writers and editors of business prose try to reduce the burden on their readers in order to satisfy Henry Fowler's objective: to make the sentences understandable on one reading (Fowler, 1926). Similarly, writing well for an E2 reader generally means using the same methods and editorial principles one uses in writing for an E1 reader— only more so. That is, one should write even simpler, clearer, easier-to-read material for the E2 reader than one writes for E1s: short familiar words, short uncomplicated sentences, active and indicative verb forms. Most of the battle in communicating with E2 readers can be won by applying George Orwell's most basic rules of style (see Orwell, 1946):

- Never use a long word where a short one will do.
- Never use a foreign phrase, a scientific word, or a jargon word if you can think of an everyday English equivalent.
- If it is possible to cut a word out, always cut it out.

As in most business and technical writing, the editor should nearly always choose the more accessible arrangement of text and figures, presuming that any facet of page design or layout that taxes the abilities or attention of an E1 reader will be an even greater burden for the E2 reader.

Sometimes, however, the needs of the E2 reader mandate new rules, such as the use of words with few meanings rather than many meanings (even when they are longer words) and sometimes longer sentences with the implied or elliptical words put back in. Often, the tactics required for this kind of communication make English documents less readable and less interesting to sophisticated E1 readers. By traditional standards, a well-written International English document is sometimes not well written. For example, consider this pair of sentences:

1. Reading is hard; writing is harder.
2. Reading is difficult; writing is more difficult than reading.

By almost any standard of editing, the first version is better written than the second. It contains not only fewer words but fewer words with more than one syllable. (Most measures of readability are based on two variables: words-per-sentence and syllables-per-word.) Version 1 is plain, direct, even slightly poetic. In contrast, the second is slow, pedestrian, and prosaic. What is more, according to the Flesch-Kincaid Readability Index, a metric used to enforce the readability standards of U.S. government documents, the first sentence requires only a third grade education to understand, while the second requires a seventh grade education.

Probably everyone from George Orwell to Strunk and White would consider the first better than the second. Yet, people who read English as their second language would probably have more trouble with the first than the second. Why?

In the first, better-written version, the key word is *hard,* a word with several meanings; a person learning English would not learn the metaphorical, "difficult" sense of *hard* first. Nor would the bilingual dictionary such a person consults list the "difficult" equivalent as the first meaning. Furthermore, the second part of the better sentence is elliptical—it leaves words out deliberately. People who speak idiomatic English know that "harder" means "harder than reading." Would someone whose English was less fluent, less idiomatic, know what was missing?

Writing in an International English Style also means removing metaphors, vogue expressions, and the kind of breezy style that characterizes much business communication. Consider this professionally written copy from a brokerage's website:

Before:

We set no boundaries on what we can accomplish with our clients. Where others see insoluble problems, we see unexpected opportunities to create new products, to introduce new technology and to enter new markets. Above all, we constantly seek to provide our clients with the timely, informed and imaginative insights necessary for them to achieve their objectives. The possibilities of today's international markets are boundless. And so is our commitment to working with our clients to seize them. You will find this spirit reflected throughout this Annual Review from the fundamentals of our firm's culture to the array of successes we helped our clients attain during 2000.
(Grade 12 Reading Difficulty)

It is difficult to simplify and clarify this text because, frankly, it consists of little more than hollow self-congratulation and untestable claims. If we revise it to make it friendlier to E2, however, it becomes:

After:
> We can accomplish much with our clients. Where others see difficult problems, we see opportunities to invent new products, to introduce new technology, and to enter new markets. Most important, we always provide our clients with the timely, intelligent, and imaginative ideas they need to succeed. The potential in today's international markets is huge. And so is our commitment to help our clients profit. This promise is in every part of this *Annual Review:* from our fundamental principles to the list of successes we helped our clients to attain in 2000.
> (Grade 11 Reading Difficulty)

Even though most E1 readers might prefer the richer style of the Before version, most E2 readers (and translators) would probably prefer the After. Granted, it is more prosaic and colorless. But it is clearer, easier to follow, and, ironically, easier to see for what it is: unsubstantiated self-praise. This explains why, generally, advertisements and corporate puffery translate poorly: they contain more sound than substance.

Generally, English meant for international business or technical consumption needs to be stripped of its humor, poesy, figures, and allusions—much of what makes reading pleasurable. Most wordplay will do nothing more than confuse or distract E2. Richard Lanham, one of the best writers on writing, represents an interesting case. In the excellent *Revising Business Prose* and several predecessor textbooks, he advocates the stripped-down, colorless approach. But in the less well-known—but far more stimulating—work, *Style: An Anti-Textbook,* written well before he saw the potential return in urging people to write colorlessly, he takes a nearly opposite view, urging business and professional writers to have as much fun with their language as they can.

The second requirement, after the need for simplification, is to *write for translation,* that is, for a reader who may consult a bilingual dictionary. Nearly every editorial decision that helps the E2 reader also helps the translator as well. Indeed, although many people who learn a new language come to think or even dream in that language, most will be translating as they read, often stopping to check a word. My international students and clients often bring a bilingual dictionary, paper or electronic, to my seminars. Writers should consider what E2s will find when they consult that dictionary.

For example, American writers are fond of the word *need* to mean "wishes" or "preferences": *create a need, meet the needs of, satisfy client needs,* or *assess training needs,* and so on. One might even argue that the use of *need* is a deliberate ploy by business writers meant to create the misimpression that there is no choice, only necessity. Unfortunately, Cassell's French-English Dictionary defines *need* as:

1. besoin (close to the meaning above, but with a greater sense of urgency or discomfort)
2. necéssité (requirement, essential)
3. adversité (a condition of threat or frustration)
4. indigence (near-poverty)

Clearly, this overworked term needs to be replaced with a more precise English synonym: create a *demand,* give the clients what they *request,* assess skill *deficiencies.* Applying this principle often reverses the most basic rule of editing: to prefer the shortest, simplest, most familiar word. Unfortunately, the short, commonplace words of English tend to have the largest number of meanings; the word *set* leads the Oxford English Dictionary in number of definitions. Thousands of basic English verbs will have a dozen or more definitions in a substantial bilingual dictionary: *make, take, fix, reach.* The problem is exacerbated when they are part of two- and three-word phrasal verbs such as *take out* or *make a fool of,* or nominalizations like *make a distinction, take a decision* (Brit.), *fix limits, reach a consensus.*

Making matters more difficult is the fact that thousands of English words can be several parts of speech. For example, *close* is noun, verb, and adjective; *closer* is noun when pronounced one way and an adjective when pronounced another.

And if that were not enough, we must also remember that when publishers issue bilingual dictionaries they will want, if possible, to use uncopyrighted, public domain editions. This means that their English definitions may be based on a dictionary 50 to 100 years old, in which the oldest meanings probably will be listed first.

Thoughtful writers will appreciate how hard it is to use bilingual dictionaries, especially those written in unfamiliar alphabets. When E2s see the English word *uncopyrighted,* for example, they might not know that it has a prefix. No English or bilingual dictionary will list the word *uncopyrighted.* What then should the writer/editor do? Select "books that are no longer copyrighted," or "un-copyrighted"? The latter choice, which solves the dictionary problem, will irritate most technical and business editors, who are forever removing unneeded hyphens from the writing of people who put "pre-test" into their drafts. Indeed, the recommendation that International English documents be punctuated aggressively, with more hyphens and commas than modern English requires or permits, generates more resistance from professional editors than any other tactic proposed in this text.

In short, sometimes the best way to write for E2 is to write for E1 with more demanding thresholds of readability and stricter tolerances. This is the style Lanham calls CBS: Clear, Brief, and Sincere. At other times, however, E2 is better served by a longer word, a nonstandard punctuation mark, or a restored elliptical word or phrase.

The Two Strategies: Culture-Free, Culture-Fair

In general, then, adapting a draft for international readers of English requires two classes of changes:

- Stripping away linguistic and cultural distractions and irritants, making the document, insofar as possible, *culture-free.*
- Adding to the document items and styles designed specifically to please and attract the local communication culture, that is, making the document *culture-fair.*

Culture-free writing is an aspect of a business and marketing strategy called *globalization*: modifying products, technologies, and the associated documents, labels, and literature so that they will be acceptable anywhere in the world in a single form. Interestingly, the globalization of a product frequently is the effect mainly of changes in communication: choices in packaging, color, illustration, branding, and language. The process is iterative, requiring feedback from readers whose sensibilities may be hard to predict, and it consists mainly in removing things that might confuse or offend—and then removing even more things.

So, a text may be globalized either as an attachment to a product, as part of globalizing the product with one-size-fits-all advertising, instructions, displays, manuals, and support websites, or as the product

itself—a book, report, proposal, stand-alone website, curriculum vi-
tae, or R&D brochure. For example, a friend who writes articles for
the gem and jewelry trade recently published a piece about heat-treated
sapphires, which he called *Blue Devils*. According to his account, a
significant number of Iranians in the New York precious stone community "went ballistic." Indeed, consider how often *devils*—a highly
charged symbol in several cultures—appear innocently as logos, mas-
cots, product names.

In any case, *globalizing* the text, at the very least, compels us to edit
out this year's vogue words ("actionable") or, in more ambitious applications, avoid constructions that start with *until*—an English construct
missing from many modern languages. Globalizing also means replacing figurative expressions with literal ones and newly-coined words with
traditional ones. It may even require the replacement of newly-coined
terms and names hard to pronounce in half the world with others that are
more easily pronounced. (People "subvocalize" to themselves while they
read; a word that is hard to pronounce—notably one starting with *r* or
th—will slow down even a silent reader.) The most extreme form of
globalization is to use a controlled form of English, a restricted vocabulary and syntax engineered specifically for clarity and simplicity. Controlled languages, as will be explained later, also facilitate machine
translation.

Globalization is a modernistic strategy seeking one-size-fits-all solutions, which, to a modernist, are also the *best practices*. Viewed favor-
ably, it is an attempt to be simple, clear, and inoffensive—all of which
are always good goals for a communicator. Looked at unfavorably, however, it is an attempt to reduce effort and save money by making one
product or document for everyone, without expending the effort or money
to adapt it to local needs or preferences.

In contrast, the postmodernistic process that leads to culture-fair communication is called *localization:* adapting a global product for local
use, or modifying a product developed for one locality so that it better
suits another, seeking a "goodness of fit" between the product/text and
the local culture.

The most obvious way to localize an English document is to translate
it into the local language of choice. How much translation, however,
usually depends on business constraints: for example, does it make sense
to have a single Portuguese translation, or separate ones for Europe and
South America?

Even when the document remains in English, however, numerous opportunities for localization present themselves. Certain cultures, for example, look with distrust at the bullet-list memo that is so popular in the United States; to localize the English version, one might change the format. Although globalization usually means removing all pictures of people from business documents, localization can entail replacing them with pictures of people who look, work, and dress like the readers.

Most of the websites concerned with localization emphasize the problem of changing the characters used on computer keyboards; yet the concept is much broader. Localizing a text with great intensity—what Nancy Hoft (1995) calls "radical localization"—can involve adapting to the particular learning styles of different reader cultures or adjusting the granularity of the information to correspond to local teaching customs.

Writing in an International English Style, then, requires a complementary use of both strategies: replacing the vogue technical term *granularity* in the previous sentence with a simpler alternative such as *level of detail* (globalization strategy), while adding a bilingual glossary of technical terms for a particular edition (localization strategy). Above all, it requires a constant awareness—and an extra iteration of editing—to ensure that E2 gets the message.

In sum, a first-draft document by an E1 writer, no matter how facile or articulate, will almost never be appropriate for an E2 reader. It will take more time to edit than most business writers are inclined to allocate. This text urges E1 writers to make the time and to appraise this use of resources as a sound investment.

Discussion Questions

- Should American business students be required to study a foreign language?
- Is it responsible for a company to send someone who speaks only English to conduct sensitive business interactions among people who do not speak English well?
- Does it matter how many languages there are in the world? Why or why not?
- In most social situations, who should adapt to whom: the host or the guest?
- Should E1s correct the language errors made by E2s?

Sources and Resources

Chaney, Lillian, and Jeanette Martin. *Intercultural Business Communication.* Englewood Cliffs, NJ: Prentice-Hall, 1995.

Crystal, David. *English as a Global Language.* Cambridge: Cambridge University Press, 1997.

Gradol, David. *The Future of English?* The British Council, 2000. (www.britishcouncil.org/learning-elt-future.pdf).

Guy, Vincent, and John Mattock. *The International Business Book.* Lincolnwood, IL: NTC Business Books, 1995.

Hoft, Nancy. *International Technical Communication.* New York: John Wiley & Sons, 1995.

Kachru, Braj B. (ed.). *The Other Tongue: English across Cultures.* 2nd ed. Chicago: University of Illinois Press, 1992.

Kirkman, John. "How Friendly Is Your Writing for Readers around the World?" In *Text, Context, and Hypertext: Writing with and for the Computer,* Edward Barrett (ed.). Cambridge, MA: MIT Press, 1988.

Lanham, Richard. *Style: An Anti-Textbook.* New Haven, CT: Yale University Press, 1974.

Lanham, Richard. *Revising Business Prose.* New York: Macmillan, 1999.

Leninger, Carol, and Rue Yuan. "Aligning International Editing Efforts with Global Business Strategies." *IEEE Transactions on Professional Communication* 41, no. 1 (March 1998): 16–23.

Orwell, George. "Politics and the English Language" (http://eserver.org/langs/politics-english-language.txt).

Strunk, William, and E.B. White. *The Elements of Style.* 4th ed. New York: Macmillan, 1995.

Thrush, Emily A. "Bridging the Gaps: Technical Communication in an International and Multicultural Society." *Technical Communication Quarterly* (Summer 1993): 271–283.

Weiss, Edmond. "Technical Communication across Cultures: Five Philosophical Questions." *Journal of Business and Technical Communication* (April 1998): 253–269.

2

Principles of Simplicity

Selecting or coining the right words can increase the chances that E2 will understand E1's writing. English has an immense vocabulary with several synonyms for most terms. Generally, writing in an International English Style *requires us to restrict our vocabulary and discipline other language choices. The objective of this chapter, therefore, is to suggest the most effective ways to replace potentially unclear vocabulary and to trim away unnecessary words.*

Meaning and Risk

People who study the techniques and troubles of verbal communication are sometimes amazed that anyone ever understands anyone else. Individual words can have a dozen meanings, only a few of them eliminated by context. Adjacent to other words, they can modify and be modified in ways the author never expected. There are even some students of language, influenced by the later philosophical investigations of Wittgenstein, who insist that no individual speaker or writer means precisely the same thing by the same word in any two utterances.

Understanding a text, even in the best of circumstances, even when everyone is an E1, requires the reader to draw inferences, make guesses, bring personal interpretations to the words. The process is known fashionably as "constructing" the text.

From the practical perspective of business and technical communication, however, much of this discourse analysis is unhelpful—except to remind us that the reader is an active participant in the writing/ reading transaction, not a passive receptacle for information. Commerce, government, and science demand that writers be understood. Even if writers cannot entirely manage and control what the readers will do with and to the text, they can at least limit the choices and reduce the opportunities for misunderstanding. In effect, making a text easy to understand usually means making it harder to misunderstand. Editing for E2s, moreover, means making it especially hard to misunderstand.

Both globalization and localization are ways of minimizing the chance that E2 will bring an interpretation to the text that is too far from the writer's intention. Obviously, because E2 has more ways to misread any string of words than E1, the need for simplicity and containing risk is even greater. The most common approach is to reduce radically the number of words and other verbal forms that may be used in the documents. So, for example, it is unwise to use the verb *to table,* which has opposite meanings in British and American English. Similarly, we should avoid *depend from,* an idiomatically correct form that is hardly ever used, and probably not use *absent* as an elliptical form of *in the absence of* ("absent any problems").

Usually, the best vocabulary choices are words E2s learn in the first few years of English study: *house,* not *domicile* or *residence; teacher,* not *instructor* or *facilitator* or even *lecturer; start*, not *initiate, initialize,* or *implement: long*, not *extended* or *protracted.* Similarly, it is usually better to use the simple, fundamental forms of the present and past tense rather than such English verb forms as the past emphatic (*he did run*), which lack equivalents in many other languages.

Taken together, these tactics—restricted vocabulary and basic verb forms—are the basis of what many call "controlled languages," artificially restricted variations of natural English meant to serve the requirements of international communication and translation. In fact, many of the recommendations in this book constitute a way of "controlling" English so as to reduce the risk of misunderstanding by E2 readers. Beyond these informal measures, however, there are also official controlled languages, institutional policies enforced throughout the company or organization, that are typically supported with software that flags deviations from the restrictions.

Ogden's Basic English

The inspiration for many simplified and limited forms of English is C.K. Ogden's Basic English, developed in the 1930s (Ogden, 1932). Ogden proposed that English should be learned and used globally. He observed that English has far fewer arcane word endings to learn than almost any other major language and that its conjugations and declensions are among the simplest. German, for example, has a gender and case inflection for every definite article, with both regular and irregular forms; English has *the*.

The main drawbacks to English as a global language, as he saw it, were its wild spelling practices and its immense vocabulary. (The shorter *Oxford English Dictionary* has 25,000 entries.) To solve the former problem, Ogden, like many language radicals of the period, including George Bernard Shaw, proposed a new set of phonetic spelling rules, so that, for example, *cough* and *cuff* would evidently end with the same sound. Not surprisingly, Ogden's spelling crusade—like everyone else's—failed. But his attack on vocabulary was far more successful.

Ogden proposed that the rich mess of English vocabulary could be reduced to 850 words, and that this tiny list, capable of being learned in a few days or weeks, could, with the application of a few consistent prefixes and suffixes, be adequate to sustain an adult level of conversation on a wide variety of personal and professional topics. Ogden's grammar recommendations and word list are widely available in books and on websites (for example, http://www.fact-index.com/b/ba/basic_english.html), but to get a sense of the vocabulary, consider the following lists, all the permitted words beginning with *u* or *y:*

- U-words—umbrella under unit up use
- Y-words—year yellow yes yesterday you young

The writer of Basic English has no *until, unless, upset,* or *usual,* as well as no *yet, yonder,* or *yoghurt.* Ogden's argument is that, somewhere in the list of 850, there is a close enough equivalent word or phrase to stand for the forbidden word—"dog doctor" for "veterinarian," for example.

Basic English, again, was more than a vocabulary. It included a restricted set of prefixes and suffixes, rules of permitted verb forms, and other techniques that would speed its learning and make it harder to misunderstand. Although some of these notions survive in newer controlled languages, what has been most retained is the word list—still used as the basic vocabulary in beginner's courses on English, especially in Asia.

Tactic 1: Adopt a Locally Invented, Controlled English

Many firms that write for an international audience elect to control the vocabulary and grammar in their documents, not just as a vague editorial goal but as a matter of enforced policy. Taking inspiration from Ogden's work, they develop a restricted vocabulary (1000 to 3000 words, plus unlimited product-specific terms, is typical) and limit the number of permissible sentence patterns. As inconvenient, even chafing, as this may be for the communicator, it radically reduces the burden on E2 and E3 readers, and especially on translators.

Beyond Ogden's foundation, these languages also learn from the higher level computing languages—like COBOL and FORTRAN—developed in the 1950s and 1960s. Instead of writing in a natural, uninhibited form of English, they use what the computer professional calls a "pseudocode," a language somewhere between ordinary English and computer code. Such artificial languages contain the following components:

- A list of approved verbs with their single definitions
- A list of approved logical operators, such as "if," "more than," and "of"
- A list of approved basic nouns
- An expandable list of new technical and product terms (mostly nouns) that may be added to accommodate the discussion of new topics, provided they can be defined with terms already in the official dictionary

The keys to implementing such a project are, first, a self-contained dictionary that uses only the terms in the controlled language, a requirement nearly impossible to meet with Ogden's 850-word list; and second, a software product that flags every deviation in the text and, like an ordinary spell checker, suggests replacements that are within the system.

As far fetched as this plan may seem to those who have never worked with such a system, it has a long history of successful application in many international companies. Caterpillar Inc. is famous in writing circles for its Ogden-influenced "Caterpillar English," an especially poetic phrase. And Kodak long ago attacked the problem of translating its film and camera product literature by creating parallel simplified versions of English and the translation languages. IBM has "Easy English," General Motors has "CASL," and Sun and Avaya (among others) have their own versions of Controlled English.

As will be explained later in this chapter, there are numerous sophisticated software products available that not only contain existing simplified and controlled versions of English, but, more important, provide the platform and tools with which to construct one's own, using the available versions as a starting point. The potential benefits for E2 readers and translators are immense. The only ones who sometimes resent controlled languages are skilled and professional communicators, who find their rules and structures nearly demeaning. Indeed, it would probably be a mistake to assign an experienced professional writer to work in such an environment—except, perhaps, as the overall supervisor and editor.

Note also that, in practice, nearly *any* word can be used in a controlled document, as long as it is defined or explained in a glossary. Although it would defeat the purpose of the method to have too many such exceptions, it also solves the problem associated with all standard methods: how to deal with the unanticipated special case.

Tactic 2: Adopt a Reduced Dictionary

Short of this extreme, one may merely adopt a limited dictionary, such as the *Beginner's Dictionary of American English Usage*, and use only words that appear in it. In Figure 2.1, for example, all the words that do not appear in the *Beginner's Dictionary* are italicized and point to synonyms that do appear in the dictionary. Those terms that do not appear in the dictionary, but are appropriate technical terminology, are boldfaced and will appear in the glossary.

Tactic 3: Adopt an Industry-Sanctioned Controlled English

Fully developed controlled languages, like *Simplified English* (SE), used internationally in the aerospace industry, even allow persons who speak English as their second language to write correct, reliable manuals and

Figure 2.1

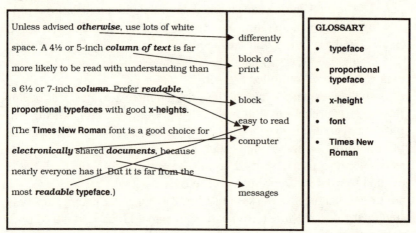

instructions in English. I have worked with E2 writers, writing in English, in an aircraft manufacturing company and have seen the impressive results they achieved in documents as sensitive as maintenance and service instructions for jet airplanes. Furthermore, those wishing to use SE, or another controlled form of English, can choose from several tools to aid the writing and editing. The following list, necessarily incomplete because of the rapid growth in this industry, is offered as introduction to the technology, without recommendation or evaluation:

- *The Boeing Simplified English Checker* (Boeing Corporation) is part of a comprehensive suite of tools, including the BSEC Vocabulary Management System and the BSEC Vocabulary Profiler.
- *Asset* (Piper Group PLC) is a tool for looking up dictionary entries and writing rules of Simplified English, as well as for updating the lexicon.
- *Cap Gemini ATS* (in the Netherlands) offers tools and services for managing a variety of controlled languages.
- *ClearCheck* (The Carnegie Group) calls itself "Controlled English Authoring and Checking Software."
- *CoAuthor* (Oracle) is an advanced terminology-management system, which includes a Simplified-English (AECMA) option.
- *Lantmaster* (LANT) is an authoring and checking product that can be combined with the same company's machine-translation system, LANTMARK.

- *SGML Language Manager* (Information Strategies Inc.) promises to help authors work within any controlled vocabulary, in AECMA Simplified English, or locally devised grammar specification.

These applications are proprietary, commercial products, used mainly by persons in the aerospace and other high-technology industries. Searching the Internet with the product names will lead to company websites and further information. Visiting www.aecma.org/publications.htm will lead you to the official (and somewhat expensive) SE papers.

Simplified English, a proprietary product, should not be confused with the Security and Exchange Commission's Plain English, a similar system meant to ensure the understandability of financial disclosure documents for all English readers. Although it has fewer rules and restrictions, it offers similar advice on style. The *SEC Plain English Handbook* can be found at www.sec.gov/pdf/handbook.pdf.

Tactic 4: Choose Words with One or Few Meanings

My relatively small German-English dictionary offers six German equivalents for the English *fix* and eleven for *mind.* Similarly, during my first European seminar, I was asked repeatedly about my unconscious and habitual use of the word *address:* as in *address a problem, address an issue, to be addressed later.* Apparently, this term mystified many members of my audience.

Ordinary English words acquire many meanings, some of them metaphorical, some of them the residue of longer expressions. In the expression *bated breath,* for example, the *bated* is a derivative of *abated.* NOTE: *Baited* is the wrong word. Not only does nearly every noun, verb, and modifier have at least two or three close synonyms, but each has a handful of meanings of its own. The word *address,* as a verb, can mean to talk about or approach; as a noun it can be a street number or a lecture. Moreover, a *lecture* can be a scholarly speech, which is synonymous with *address,* or a scolding, which is not.

Simplified English systems, of course, address (I mean solve) this problem by artificially limiting each word to a single meaning AND a single part of speech. The SE glossary is compact, and each entry resolves questions of meaning. In contrast, a standard dictionary, especially a large one, offers numerous possibilities, more questions than answers. To illustrate, here is the SE definition of *head:*

Head (n)–the top of something.

In contrast, *The American Heritage Dictionary* (4th ed.) offers 32 definitions of *head* as a noun, including an obscene one. Fortunately, the *American Heritage* lists the most recent definitions first; its first definition, however, contains the word *forwardmost,* a term that will appear in almost no dictionary and registers as a spelling error for my word processor. There are also four definitions of *head* as an adjective, including a slang reference to users of illegal drugs, six as a transitive verb, and three as an intransitive verb.

Although few bilingual dictionaries are so extensive in their definitions, it is still extremely useful for E1 writers to acquire bilingual dictionaries for the main languages of their E2 readers and to check a sample of their nouns and verbs. When several meanings of the English word are given, writers should either choose a word whose definition is first or second, or, alternately, choose another word. To illustrate, the Cassell's French-English dictionary does not offer a definition of *address* close to my meaning in *address a problem;* the closest it comes is *entreprendre,* to address oneself to. The Oxford Hebrew-English Dictionary offers seven Hebrew synonyms for the transitive verb *address,* none of them as close as the French.

If, however, the writer replaces *address the problem* with *explain the problem,* the result is much better. Here Cassell's offers one French synonym for *explain*—*expliquer*—which is quite close to the meaning; the Oxford Hebrew gives three synonyms for *explain,* but the first, reading from the right, is *l'havhir,* which is the closest to the intended meaning. As a recurring editorial tactic, then, writers should replace a word with many meanings with one that has fewer meanings, or only one, in rare cases.

But what if there is no such alternative? Obviously, the solution is to select a word whose first or second meaning comes closest to your intention. This rule can be difficult to follow, however. Unfortunately, many of the world's dictionaries still honor the policy of listing the *oldest* meanings of a word first, not mentioning the current meanings until the end of the entry. So, the first three or four definitions may be rare or archaic!

Indeed, throughout the world, it is difficult to know what English dictionary has been used as the basis for the English component of the bilingual dictionary. Often, it may be assumed that the text is from a public domain edition, hopelessly out of date. That assumption is for those countries that honor American copyrights; in other countries, a more recent dictionary might have been plagiarized. The public domain version of Webster's Unabridged (1913)—the basis of many no-royalty English dictionaries—illustrates the problem. If you look up *transparent,* you will find

> (Trans*par"ent) *a.* [F., from LL. *transparens, -entis,* p. pr. of *transparere* to be transparent; L. *trans* across, through + *parere* to appear.)
> 1. Having the property of transmitting rays of light, so that bodies can be distinctly seen through; pervious to light; diaphanous; pellucid; as, *transparent* glass; a *transparent* diamond;— opposed to *opaque.* "*Transparent* elemental air." *Milton.*
> 2. Admitting the passage of light; open; porous; as, a *transparent* veil. *Dryden.*

For *template,* this dictionary says "Same as Templet," and for *templet* the dictionary says

> (Tem'plet) n. [LL. templatus vaulted, from L. templum a small timber.] [Spelt also template.]
> 1. A gauge, pattern, or mold, commonly a thin plate or board, used as a guide to the form of the work to be executed; as, a mason's or a wheelwright's templet.
> 2. (Arch.) A short piece of timber, iron, or stone, placed in a wall under a girder or other beam, to distribute the weight or pressure.

In other words, any bilingual dictionary based on this lexicon (or its derivatives) will probably be no help to an E2 reader confronting the modern uses of *transparent* or *template.* That is all the more reason to replace words that are current and fashionable, where possible, with more traditional, stable vocabulary (*invisible, open,* or *obvious* for *transparent; pattern, format,* or *design* for *template*).

The problems of word choice illustrate why, as mentioned earlier, the special needs of E2 often oblige us to use longer words with more syllables than we would use in writing for E1. Most E1s know what we mean when we say, succinctly, that *an investigate trail is cold.* Most E2s can barely guess, and their bilingual dictionaries will get them no closer.

Tactic 5: Avoid Verbs with Two or Three Words in Them (Phrasal Verbs)

When possible, we should replace two-word verbs like *look at* or *carry on* with *examine* or *continue*. We probably should not replace *carry on* with the verb *resume,* however, since it has several meanings and would lead the reader to an unnecessarily complicated dictionary entry.

Although most advice on international communication recommends short familiar words, often such basic verbs as *make, take, have, set,* and others can have scores of context-dependent meanings. International readers will have trouble with *make a difference* versus *make progress* versus *make sense.* Consider the following:

- take charge
- take issue
- take offense
- take one's turn
- take a turn for the worse
- take out (go on a date)
- take out (destroy or neutralize)

Of course, if we are using a simplified or controlled vocabulary, words like *tolerate* might not appear in the controlled vocabulary, forcing us to use the two-word form.

Instead of . . .	Try
Open up	Expand, enlarge
Shut out	Prevent, prohibit
Carry on	Continue
Speak to	Discuss
Make clear	Clarify, explain
Follow up	Pursue, track

Also avoid three-word verbs like *put up with* or *make a fool of;* prefer *tolerate* or *embarrass.*

Instead of . . .	Try
Take offense at	Resent
Keep abreast of	Monitor, assess
Beat up on	Abuse, overwhelm
Take advantage of	Exploit

There are numerous compendiums of phrasal verbs on the Internet. A good example is Dennis Oliver's Phrasal Verb Page, http://eslcafe.com/pv/pv-mng.html.

By replacing two- and three-word verbs with prepositional tails, we solve another editorial problem as well: *to-which, of-which,* and *with-which.* The misguided attempt to impose Latin grammar on English (which is a Germanic language) has led to the notion that sentences may not end with prepositions and therefore coerced otherwise good writers to offer such clumsy sentences as: *The report outlines three problems to which we should attend.* This prissy sentence structure overlooks the fact that the verb is *attend to;* more important, it generates a sentence with a noticeably un-English word pattern and increases the difficulty for E2. Replacing the two-word verb *attend to* with a one word substitute like *discuss* eliminates the problem.

Tactic 6: Use the Simplest Verb Forms

Many of the tactics in this chapter have the common objective of increasing the chance that the English we write for E2 will use the vocabulary and grammar learned in the early years of English instruction. And, as everyone who has studied a foreign language remembers, it often takes many years to learn the more advanced and complicated forms of the verbs: difficult tenses, voices, and moods.

For that reason, we can simplify the task of E2 if we avoid, wherever possible, the emphatic and progressive English tenses. Instead of *we will be arriving,* use *we will arrive.* Instead of *Do you have,* use *Have you.* (Some forms of controlled English severely restrict the use of words ending in *ing* because of the several problems associated with this suffix.)

Before:
- The first screen asks whether you will be using the same password.
- ROI corporation was managing our overseas distribution.
- The system has been extensively improved since Release 1.

After:
- The first screen asks: Will you use the same password?
- ROI corporation managed our overseas distribution.
- Release 2 is considerably better than Release 1.

Again, it is best to prefer verb forms in the order students of foreign language generally learn them: active before passive; indicative before subjunctive. The passive voice is at least as dangerous in International English as in all other writing; sentences that start with, for example, *it has been determined that* may never recover.

Before:
- Vacation dates are usually decided by the Human Resources administrator.
- If access to the building is denied, the security officer must be contacted.
- With the online banking option, overdrafts are covered automatically.

After:
- The Human Resources administrator usually decides vacation dates.
- If you cannot enter the building, contact the security officer.
- The online banking option covers overdrafts automatically.

For similar reasons, it is better to use the indicative mood than the subjunctive. Granted, except for flight attendant speeches (*Should your future travel plans*) the subjunctive is nearly missing from most American business writing. Now and then, however, it bursts through in such expressions as *should it prove to be the case that* (*if*) or *should you decide to* (*if you decide to*).

Before:
Should access to your files *be* denied, the system administrator must be notified.

After:
If the network denies you access to your files, notify the system administrator.

Tactic 7: Define Many Terms in a Glossary

International English documents should generally include a glossary of all coined, new, difficult, technical, or otherwise unfamiliar terms. For those using a controlled English system, any term not in the official lexicon *must* be defined in a glossary, which uses terms from the approved word list to define the term. Any word in the glossary should be highlighted in the text, through some special typography or color. The oldest and most widely used convention in technical publications is to boldface all terms in the glossary and use boldface for no other purpose. This gives the reader, E1 or E2, an immediate sense of how much new or difficult vocabulary is on a given page.

The traditional way of presenting glossaries is as an attachment or appendix at the end of the document. Unfortunately, asking readers to branch and loop through a document lowers the general attractiveness and usefulness of the publication. Indeed, when one leaves the main text to pursue a definition in the glossary, it is often difficult to work one's way back to the original point of departure. The more the intended reader of a document is asked to read anything other than the next word, the greater the burden, the less reliable the communication, the less attractive the publication, and the more likely that the reader will abandon the process.

The best way to define unfamiliar or difficult text is immediately, within the line in which the novel term appears. This minimizes branching and searching. Most organizations that publish legal and technical publications aspire to spell out and explain new terms this way *the first time they appear,* especially if they are acronyms or abbreviations. Thereafter, the reader is expected to rely on the glossary. But there are two problems with this method:

- When a publication is long and complicated, readers rarely read it straight through, so that the first time they see a new term may not be the first time it appears in the text.
- Any page in any document is likely to be cut and pasted into any other document from the same organization, with no attempt to spell out, within the body of the text, the meanings of terms defined elsewhere in the original.

Therefore, I recommend as the best approach a dynamic glossary that defines the new and difficult terms in a footnote area at the bottom of each page (or at the end of each two-page spread). (See Figure 2.2.)

Although asking readers to branch to the bottom of the page and back can be somewhat distracting, it is far more comfortable a method than sending readers to the end of the publication or the back of the book. Moreover, if the definitions are stored with the file as footnotes, they will travel with the passage in which they appear and be retained in the next document that uses that material.

The problem of glossaries at the end of the publication, like many problems of book design and copy fitting, is effectively solved with hypertext. The ideal way to communicate in English with E2 is to engineer a file to be read on the computer screen, in which glossary definitions

Figure 2.2   **Dynamic Glossary for One-Sided Publications (A) and Two-Sided Publications (B)**

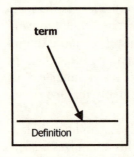
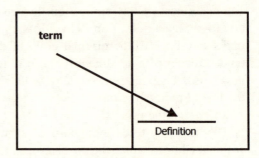

A. One-Page Unit   B. Two-Page Spread (Double Sided)

can be accessed by "mousing over" the text in question. In fact, International English in hypertext can be even more effective by linking itself to online dictionaries in several languages, so that any word in the text can activate an entry from a dictionary in the first language of the reader. Although this technology will solve few of the substantive dictionary or meaning problems discussed in this chapter and elsewhere, it will at least make life easier for E2s and encourage them to read documents that would otherwise be too burdensome.

These are, of course, expensive and time-consuming adaptations. But they may be justifiable in circumstances where the costs of misunderstanding are extremely high, or the potential for profit exceeds the cost.

Tactic 8: Choose Words that Are Pronounceable

When people read silently to themselves, they speak the words they are reading in their minds and typically hear them in their own voice. The phenomenon is called *subvocalization*. This link between silent reading and speech can be problematical. For example, most people cannot read any faster than they can speak; those who wish to break through this speed barrier must force themselves to quit the subvocalization habit, even to the point of no longer reading words in sequence.

For writers of International English, the persistence of subvocalization means that hard-to-pronounce words will be hard to read, to the point of slowing the reader and interrupting the flow of ideas. This observation is particularly germane when naming products, systems, or companies, the situation in which writers may have their greatest freedom in choosing or inventing words. For example, nearly every E2 has trouble with the *th* sound (especially unvoiced, as in *with*), and many E2s from Asian countries struggle with *l* and *r*. When General Instrument Corporation of Horsham, Pennsylvania, changed its image in 1996, it also adopted the more high-tech-sounding name of *NextLevel*. In 1998, it restored the original name, mainly because most of its Asian customers for cable-TV converter boxes had trouble with saying the *l* in NextLevel. Similarly, the spokesclown for McDonald's restaurants in Japan is called *Donald McDonald* not *Ronald,* out of consideration for Japanese customers who have difficulty with *r*.

When creating names, especially names based on product or system acronyms, it is also useful to make sure that the newly created word does not have some unpleasant or unintended meaning in the first language of some segment of your E2 readers. Newly coined product names should be checked by persons who speak Spanish, Mandarin, Hindi/ Urdu, and other major languages spoken among the audience. It would be unfortunate if the new name, though easily pronounceable, embarrassed your company or organization by being bizarre or off-color in one of these languages.

Tactic 9: Do not Coin Words that Are not Needed

Coining words and inventing new technical terms is one of the more enjoyable parts of writing. But only those with a keen knowledge of English and an especially good ear for its nuances should try it. Nothing is to be gained, especially if the audience is E2, by coining a word for a situation in which a perfectly good English word already exists. And only someone with more than a casual knowledge of the language can be sure, before coining or inventing a new word, that there is not already a suitable English word in the dictionary. For example, many years ago someone without such awareness introduced *prioritize* into our discourse—an ugly, pretentious, and unnecessary substitute for the verb *rank*. Similarly, English has no need for the verb *mentored* (*taught* or *guided*) and certainly no need for the absurd *mentee* (*student, apprentice, protégé*). Equally confounding is the invention of pseudotechnical terminology, like *visioning process* for *planning*. What could be more obvious than the proposition that E2s will have considerable difficulty understanding words and phrases that the E1 just invented, terms they have never heard in school, never read in books, never seen anywhere before. How can anyone expect E2 to deduce that the silly *mentee* is a back formation from the vogue word *mentor?*

Another reason that coining words requires an unusually deep knowledge of English is that one must be sure that the so-called new word does not in fact already exist with an established meaning of its own. Over the past twenty years, more and more speakers in business and government have decided that the word *actionable* means practical, feasible, and susceptible to action or intervention. In this use, an actionable recommendation is one that can be followed. "Actionable intelligence," to use the latest popular variation on this word, is information reliable enough that you can take dangerous actions based on it.

Unfortunately, the word *actionable* already has a well-established dictionary meaning: "just cause for a lawsuit." Any attorney will tell you that a person who does something actionable will be sued and will probably lose the lawsuit. Obviously, the language never needed this variant meaning of *actionable*. Actionable recommendations are just feasible or practicable recommendations. Actionable intelligence is trustworthy intelligence (as opposed to the regular kind). And, most important for this discussion, now *actionable* cannot be used reliably in any business communication, especially one aimed at E2.

This is not to suggest that words cannot change their meanings. In fact, words add and change meanings perpetually. Rather, the point is that not all language change adds clarity or precision to communication and, moreover, that words in a transition of meaning usually do not belong in International English documents. To illustrate, an E2 reader consulting a bilingual dictionary will read that *enormity* is a synonym for *atrocity* (not *immensity*) and that *fortuitous* means *accidental* (not *lucky*). It avails little that the E1 who used those words meant something else by them and that most Americans would have understood them with meanings not in that dictionary.

Tactic 10: Avoid Redundant and Wordy Expressions for Time and Place

Business and technical documents are never more long-winded and wordy than in expressing simple matters of time, space, distance, or sequence. *At this point in time* is one of fifty long-winded ways to say *now* or *currently*. Whole volumes of these replacements are in print, and many are incorporated into the style-checking programs of word processors. See, for example, Steven Wilbers's webpage, http://www.wilbers.com/Keys1Exercises.htm, or my own book, *100 Writing Remedies* (1990).

This sort of verbosity is understandable and acceptable in impromptu speaking, and even in hastily composed first drafts. But it should not survive the first draft. A productive way to reduce the burden on E2 is to trim these expressions to their leanest forms, especially the redundant ones like *3 square meters of area.*

Time Wasters

Instead of . . .	Use
two weeks' duration	two weeks
period of time	time, period
interval of time	interval
twenty-minute period	twenty minutes
three hours long	three hours
during periods of time	during
three hours of time	three hours

The expressions "calendar month" and "calendar year" are necessary only to distinguish your meaning from "person-month" or "staff- year"; also avoid the expression "time frame"—a phrase with such various simple meanings as *due date, deadline,* or *interval.*

Before:
Adding new security points to the terminal, which will require a period of three months' construction, cannot be done under your time frame.

After:
Adding new security points to the terminal, which will require three months' construction, cannot be completed by your deadline.

Place Wasters

Instead of . . .	Use
2 meters in length	2 meters long
3 feet in height	3 feet high
10 square feet of space	10 square feet
15 square meters of area	15 square meters
3 cubic yards of volume	3 cubic yards
distance of 4 kilometers	4 kilometers (away)
in a westward direction	westward

Before:
Office buildings shall not be more than 100 meters in height.
After:
Office buildings shall not be more than 100 meters high.

Before:
The inspectors are traveling from a location 2,000 miles away.
After:
The inspectors are traveling 2,000 miles.

Tactic 11: Avoid Unhelpful Redundancies

In high-risk communication through noisy or unreliable channels, saying things two or three times can be very helpful; we expect pilots to repeat remarks spoken through distorted radio channels, for example. Other forms of redundancy, like beginning a report with a summary of the findings, or showing statistics in both text and charts, increase the chance of communicating with a large or diverse audience. Indeed, those who study the statistics of information understand that saying a thing twice squares the chance that the message will get through, and saying it three times cubes the chance.

This useful redundancy should not be confused, however, with useless redundancy, phrases in which the redundancy merely slows or muddies the conversation.

Instead of . . .	Use
rectangular in shape	rectangular
visible to the eye	visible
past history	past or history
entirely finished	finished
midway between	between
completely finished	finished, complete
totally dedicated	dedicated
totally devoted	devoted

There is no such thing, of course, as *somewhat dedicated* or *partially devoted.*

Also be mindful of what Winston Churchill called "adverbial dressing gowns," writing *utterly reject* when *reject* will do or *thoroughly understand* when *understand* makes the point better. Another excellent compendium of tactics for controlling wordiness and redundancy is Brogan (1973). Despite the age of the text, it has never been improved upon, and despite the title it is for *everyone* who writes, not just those writing about science and technology.

Tactic 12: Avoid Nominalizations

Unfortunately, there are many times in school and business when writers are encouraged to make their writing as wordy and technical-sounding as possible. Those who succeed at this misrepresentation usually rely on *nominalization*, a process that converts a powerful, direct verb like *decide* into a weak, pseudotechnical expression like *reach a decision with respect to*. Nominalizations (sometimes called "smothered verbs") are endemic to legal testimony, political press conferences, social sciences, and all other discourse in which the goal is to make ordinary commentary sound more like scientific or technical reporting. They are also popular with people who need to break bad news; somehow, it is argued, *We have not yet made a selection regarding a project leader* sounds less disappointing or incompetent than *We have not yet selected a project leader.*

Many writers and speakers use these constructions incessantly. The clearest evidence is the repetition of the *-tion* and *-ment* suffix at the ends of nouns. (I sometimes tell my clients that smothered verbs make a "shun" sound when they are choking.)

For anyone new to English, nominalizations are perplexing, especially those in the passive voice ("no decision has been reached with respect to"); they are like the multi-word, phrasal verbs mentioned above, in that they lead the reader on fruitless dictionary searches. In general, very few should survive the first draft of a document meant for E2 readers.

The most basic category of smothered verb is a phrase beginning with *have* or *make.*

Instead of . . .	Use
have an objection	object
have knowledge of	know
have reservations about	doubt
have a suspicion	suspect
have a concern	care, worry
make a distinction	distinguish, differentiate
make a recommendation	recommend
make a suggestion	suggest
make a proposal	propose

Before:
We did not have sufficient knowledge of the problem to make a proposal regarding a solution.
After:
We did not know enough about the problem to propose a solution.

Smothered verbs can be formed in many ways. Although the most common forms use *have* and *make,* there are also hundreds of expressions using such words as *give, reach,* and *do.*

Instead of . . .	Use
give an answer to	answer
give an apology	apologize
give a justification for	justify
reach a conclusion	conclude
reach a decision regarding	decide
reach an end	end, finish
reach an agreement	agree
do an inspection of	inspect, check
do a draft of	draft
raise an objection	object
hold the opinion	believe
send an invitation to	invite
hold a meeting	meet
furnish an explanation for	explain
furnish a solution for	solve
form a plan regarding	plan

Before:
These receipts furnish no explanation for your expenses.
After:
These receipts do not explain your expenses.

Before:
We held a meeting and reached a decision to send him an invitation to the bidders' conference.
After:
We met and decided to invite him to the bidders' conference.

The writing of technical professionals, and especially of those who aspire to seem more scientific and analytical than they really are, makes use of an especially ornate and complicated form of smothered verb, using such words as *accomplish, achieve, realize,* or even *effectuate.*

Instead of . . .	Use
exhibit improvement	improve
demonstrate success	succeed
constitute a replacement	replace
effectuate a system start-up	start up the system
evidence size reduction	shrink, reduce

To make things worse, this last group often appears in the passive voice of the verb.

Instead of . . .	Use
separation was effectuated	they separated
change was exhibited	they changed
a profit was realized	they profited
file linkage was achieved	we linked the files

Before:
A tendency to overheat was evidenced by these monitors.
After:
These monitors tended to overheat.

Before:
The calculations to project interim revenues are accomplished entirely in TREND module.
After:
The TREND module projects the interim revenues.

The examples below illustrate what are probably the most widely used nominalizations. Be especially alert to them:

Before (serve):
This report serves to explain the three stages of the project.
After:
This report explains the three stages of the project.

Before (use):
The Backspace key is used to correct errors on the screen.
After:
The Backspace key corrects errors on the screen.

Before (conduct):
The agency will conduct an investigation of the incident.
After:
The agency will investigate the incident.

Before (carry out):
Can we carry out the inspection of this disposal site before November?
After:
Can we inspect this disposal site before November?

Before (perform):
Comparison of the actual and forecast return is performed within the software.
After:
The software compares the actual return with the forecast.

Obviously, these wordy, even tortuous expressions are supposed to impress readers. (They do not, of course.) They certainly add an unnecessary portion of complexity and difficulty to the burden of the E2 reader.

Discussion Questions

- Is easily understood writing more or less impressive to most readers than difficult and obscure writing? Under what conditions?
- Should student projects be assigned a minimum length, number of words, or pages?
- Is there some other way to measure the level of student effort?
- Can one write simply without writing down or condescending to the reader?
- Would E2 readers resent the claim that ordinary English needs to be simplified for them?

Sources and Resources

AECMA (Association Europeene de Constructeurs de Materiel Aerospatial). "AECMA Simplified English Standard." Brussels, Belgium: AECMA Doc.PSC-85–6598, Issue I, 1995.

Brogan, John. *Clear Technical Writing*. New York: McGraw-Hill, 1973.

Collin, P., M. Lowi, and Weiland, C. *Beginner's Dictionary of American English Usage, Second Edition*. New York: McGraw-Hill, 2002.

Ogden, C.K. *Basic English, a General Introduction with Rules and Grammar*. London: Paul Trebor & Co, 1932.

Thomas, Margaret, Gloria Jaffee, J. Peter Kincaid, and Yvette Stees. "Learning to Use Simplified English: A Preliminary Study." *Technical Communication* 39 (1992).

U.S. Securities and Exchange Commission. *Plain English Handbook.* (www.sec.gov/pdf/handbook.pdf)

Weiss, Edmond. *100 Writing Remedies.* Scottsdale, AZ: Greenwood/Oryx Press, 1990.

Weiss, Edmond. "Twenty-Five Tactics to 'Internationalize' Your English." *Intercom* (January 1998) 11–15.

Wilbers, S. *Steven Wilbers' Webpage,* http://www.wilbers.com

3

Principles of Clarity

Clarity is mainly a property of sentences and paragraphs. Clearly written passages anticipate the ways in which they would be misunderstood, eliminating phrases and constructions that are likely to mislead or confuse the reader while, at the same time, providing emphasis and guides. Skillful writers and editors avoid the two ways of being unclear: passages that befuddle the reader and, worse, ambiguous passages that can be legitimately misinterpreted. The objective of this chapter, therefore, is to caution against those ways of associating and stringing words most likely to confuse or mislead E2.

The Problem: Clear Only If Known

Writers can never be entirely sure their writing is clear and unambiguous. Our own writing is nearly always clear to ourselves. We perceive transitions that are missing, emphases that are lacking, and explanations that are wanting. We gloss over the clumsy passages and always choose the correct way out of the ambiguities.

I usually think of a clear passage (sentence or paragraph) as one in which a reader who knows the meanings of all the individual words will also grasp the intended meaning of the passage, preferably on one fairly effortless reading. Oddly, however, individually clear words can become confusing when in difficult combinations or odd positions, especially when read by an E2 reader unfamiliar with the subtle rules of English word sequence or the meaning of certain utterly illogical idiomatic expressions.

For example, in the introduction to this book, I found myself writing *opportunities for misunderstanding,* but realized that, for E2 the interpretation of *opportunity* in this phrase is itself an opportunity for misunderstanding. And in the sentence above, *I found myself writing* would be far easier to interpret as *I wrote.*

To appreciate how difficult and elusive clear writing can be, consider this simple example, which is part of Newton's Law of Gravity: *Every particle of matter in the universe attracts every other particle.* For many years, I believed this sentence to be a model of clarity. I argued that anyone who understood the meaning of each word would inevitably understand the sentence—that is, until a client pointed out that *every other* has two meanings in English: all others and every second (or alternating, as in We meet *every other* Thursday). Now, look at the sentence again: *Every particle of matter in the universe attracts every other particle.* See its meaning move in and out like one of those reversible optical illusions.

Of course, some will object that my example is far-fetched, that no sensible person could possibly believe the universe is so constructed that each particle attracts every second particle. And that is the point: Only if you know independently what the sentence means can you guess the correct path out of the ambiguity. Editors call the phenomenon *Clear Only If Known* (COIK).

Suppose the sentence were: *On Mondays they service the front office terminals; on Thursdays they service every other terminal.* The point is that *every other* should be replaced with *all other,* making it far harder to reach a defensible misreading.

Every other illustrates several problems that complicate E2's reading experience: an arbitrary idiom, a pair of words whose meaning could not be discerned by looking up the words individually in a dictionary, and a single phrase with more than one meaning.

Outside of literature, it is unwise to expect that the reader will pause and decipher the ambiguity in a passage. The mere fact that there are contextual clues is not reason to think that the reader will do the necessary detective work.

Tactic 13: Be Careful of Loosely Connected Words and Phrases

English is one of the uninflected languages, relying more on word order than on grammatically meaningful word endings. In fact, one of the few English inflections—*who* versus *whom*—is too hard for the average American speaker to learn. This characteristic, one that caused Ogden to propose English as an international language, means that the sequence of words becomes more important to the meaning.

In general, descriptive words, phrases, and clauses will modify the noun or verb they are nearest to; putting words in the wrong position will cause unintended associations that are either confusing or funny. Most editors and writers have amassed collections of the more absurd ones:

- After eating my lunch, the project director reassigned me.
- I have resumes for the four accountants on my desk.
- Transfers should not be given to commuters until they have been punched.
- The patient left the hospital urinating freely.

An E1 speaker will make allowances for these dangling constructions and misplaced phrases that occur commonly in unedited business documents, especially in instructions. But E2 readers, applying the rules they learned in school, may be baffled. To internationalize your English, then, be especially wary of loosely connected, dangling phrases at either the beginning or end of a sentence. The rule is simple: phrases based on participles (for example, *eating*) and infinitives (for example, *to eat*) must be connected in meaning to nearby words. An introductory phrase should refer to the word or phrase right after the comma; an ending phrase should refer to the word or phrase before the comma.

If, for example, a sentence begins *Hoping for an earlier delivery,* then the next word or phrase in the sentence is the person or group who is hoping.

Before (participle):
Hoping for an earlier delivery date, a new carrier was selected.

(Who was hoping?)

After:
> Hoping for an earlier delivery date, they engaged a new carrier.

Equally prone to this error are sentences starting with infinitives.

Before (infinitive):
> To ensure a wide market, ISO 9000 registration will be included in the plan.

(Who is ensuring?)

After:
> To ensure a wide market, we shall include ISO 9000 registration in the plan.

Dangling and misplaced phrases occur much too regularly in technical manuals and business procedures, especially those containing contingencies and dependencies. Although the ranks of professional technical communicators have grown since the 1980s, I suspect that the typical computer-related instruction is still being written by someone with no ear for (or training in) clear technical communication. Insensitivity to danglers and overreliance on passive verbs gives us such sentences as:

Before:
- To conserve energy, monitors should be turned off at the end of the day.
- When updating the file, other programs should be closed.
- After reconciling the transaction log, a report should be prepared by the analyst.

After:
- To conserve energy, (you should) turn off your monitor at the end of the day.
- When updating the file, (you must) close all other programs.
- After reconciling the transaction log, the analyst should prepare a report.

Many procedures and instructions also contain dangling phrases at their ends; the authors wanted to modify the whole sentence (called an absolute construction), but the temperament of English syntax causes the phrase to modify the last noun instead.

Before:
   Run the end-of-day routine, keeping the usual offline copy.
After:
   When you run the end-of-day routine, (you must) keep the usual offline copy.

Tactic 14: Be Aware of Frequently Misplaced Descriptive Words

Any descriptive word or phrase will modify what it is nearby, whether or not the author intended it. But the most frequently misplaced modifiers, the most slippery words in English, are the commonplace terms *only, nearly,* and *almost.* In the absence of inflections, E2 will be forced to guess what is being modified, a process made even more difficult when there are two or more candidates to choose among.

Only is probably the most frequently misplaced. What, for example, should be understood from the sentence: *The inspectors will only leave the site after all five tests.* The author of the sentence is quite sure that it is clear and does not realize that it predicts that the inspectors will "only leave," whatever that means. Depending on the intended emphasis the sentence should read either:

   • The inspectors will leave the site only after all five tests.
   • Only after all five tests will the inspectors leave the site.

(Some editors might prefer *The inspectors will stay on site until the last test is run*, but, as already mentioned, *until* is a difficult construct in many languages.)

In the best case, a misplaced *only* will lead to a bit of confusion and extra work for E2; in the worst case, it can lead to a misreading of the meaning of the sentence. Changing the position of *only* can frequently alter the meaning of the sentence.

   • Only graduates of MIT will receive on-site interviews.
   • Graduates of only MIT will receive on-site interviews.
   • Graduates of MIT will receive only on-site interviews.

Although many business and technical editors tend to cut the *only* from these and similar sentences, arguing that it is an unnecessary word, this is usually a mistake. The following sentences are not equivalent in meaning:

- We have two openings in the internship program.
- We have only two openings in the internship program.

The pursuit of simplicity and clarity should not entail the elimination of emphasis and evaluation from business sentences. Only a trivial portion of international business and technical communication is concerned exclusively with facts (we have two openings). Indeed, this portion, comprising simple facts, is best communicated in simple lists and tables. The material requiring full sentences and paragraphs must contain words and phrases that highlight and underscore—language that must be edited carefully so that E2s accustomed to inflected languages will understand.

Again, although *only* is the most frequently misplaced, *nearly* (or *approximately*) and *almost* occur in the wrong location nearly as often. (NOTE: I did not write nearly occur as often.)

Before:
- They nearly bought the entire supply of lumber.
- This year's conference almost received the highest number of applications.

After:
- They bought nearly the entire supply of lumber.
- This year's conference received almost the highest number of applications.

Tactic 15: Do not Confuse Frequently Confused Terms

When foreign languages are taught in school, the first objective is to cover the basics of vocabulary and grammar. Soon thereafter, however, teachers begin the long process of introducing the irregularities: eccentric verb forms, strange idioms, correct usages that break the rules they have just taught. It is not surprising, then, that E2 readers—who have been drilled in school on the differences between *like* and *as,* the proper form of *effect* and *affect,* the conjugation of the verbs *lie* and *lay* and other tricky parts of everyday English—avoid these errors that are so common in the writing of E1s. The least that E1 writers can do is get their own grammar right!

Before:
- Like we said at the meeting, this change order will not effect the price.
- This is no time to lay down on the job.

After:
- As we said at the meeting, this change order will not affect the price.
- This is no time to lie down on the job.

Nowadays, this problem of using the wrong word is compounded both by a decline in serious reading among educated adults and an overreliance on the spell-checking/style-checking software in our word processors. But most software programs cannot know that you used the wrong *compliment* or *principle*. They certainly do not know when you meant *affect,* rather than *effect.* Among the many frequently confused words, be especially aware of words the spell checker cannot differentiate:

- accept/except
- affect/effect
- alright/all right
- already/all ready
- canvass/canvas
- compliment/complement
- counsel/council
- devise/device
- discrete/discreet (almost no business writers understand this distinction)
- fourth/forth
- foreword/forward
- immanent/imminent/eminent
- its/it's (probably the most common mechanical error in all writing)
- peak/pique
- pore/pour
- principal/principle
- stationary/stationery
- than/then
- their/there/they're
- too/to/two
- waive/wave

This list is short; there are hundreds of homophonic (sound-alike) English words with different spellings. (To see a list with hundreds of homophones, visit Alan Cooper's page: http://www.cooper.com/alan/

homonym_list.html.) Remember that spell-checkers do not actually check spelling; rather, they compare your string of characters with a list of acceptable strings. If your misspelling happens to be an actual word (like *desert* for *dessert*), the spell checker finds no error. This is true not only for the homophonic terms above, but also for all sorts of typing mistakes that yield real words: *wok* for *work; fro* for *for; morn* for *norm.*

We must also be aware of what the dictionary calls "variant" spellings; these tend to be widely used misspellings that are gradually gaining acceptability—for example, *supercede* instead of the correct *supersede*. The problem is that variant spellings, like variant meanings, have probably not yet made their way into the bilingual dictionaries and texts on English as a Second Language. Indeed, one may guess that most international instruction is still teaching students that *supersede* is among the most frequently misspelled words in English (the only word ending with *sede*), even though the Microsoft Word spell checker now accepts the incorrect, and etymologically absurd, *supercede.*

Tactic 16: Form Words in Standard Ways

One word may be formed into many, usually by applying a set of rules peculiar to the language. Small children learning English will, with fascinating predictability, form *catched* and *mouses* by applying these elemental rules, and only later learn the irregular forms. Similarly, when *bringed* does not work, they will try *brang* before *brought.* One of the recurring themes in the recent literature on cognitive and language development is an analysis of this so-called grammar engine, which—according to the leading school these days—is hardwired at birth into the human organism. The most persuasive case for this notion is in Steven Pinker's *Words and Rules* (1999).

The practice of forming new words out of old ones continues throughout life, with uneven results. E1 writers should be aware of illegitimate *back formations*, as they are called, which lead to such errors as *administrate* (for *administer*) and *orientate* (for *orient*). And all writers, especially those trying to communicate with E2 readers, should resist the temptation to form imponderable words such as *impactful.* Generally, one should not coin a word if a perfectly good word already exists; *impactful* can be replaced by *effective, potent, powerful, successful,* or whatever the author means by this meaningless term. Here are some other potentially confusing formations:

NO	YES
remediate	remedy, cure, repair
detainee	prisoner
attendee	participant, student, client
enthused	enthusiastic, optimistic
deselect	reject, decline
graphic	graphical, pictorial
mentee	student, protégé, trainee

Sometimes, two forms exist with different meanings; the verb *to repair* gives us two noun forms—*repairs* and *reparations,* words with different meanings.

Tactic 17: Use Standard Spellings

Avoid clever nonstandard spellings, frequently associated with commercial advertising: *lite, nite, creme, kreme.* Also use more traditional, conservative spellings: for example, *dialogue*, rather than *dialog*. And, of course, if your E2 audience prefers British to American English, you might need to make those spelling adjustments as well. To illustrate:

American	British
honor	honour
memorize	memorise
fulfill	fulfil
analog	analogue
bank	banque
check	cheque
judgment	judgement
license	licence
program	programme
traveling	travelling
learned	learnt
forecast	forecasted
lit	lighted

Tactic 18: Avoid Converting Nouns into Verbs

Refrain from "verbing" nouns, although that is where many English verbs—including *dial, print, table,* and *type*—originate. Do not expect E2 to know what you mean when you *source* something or your foreign software collaborator to guess what is involved in *defeaturizing* a software release. Resist the temptation to describe your payment plan as *incentivized* or your office design as *cubicled!*

In the preceding examples, the use of verb endings at least gives E2 a clue to the meaning of the formation. E2 will probably have even greater difficulty with the following nouns used without verb endings as verbs:

Critique	(criticize, assess)
Mentor	(teach, train, guide)
Lawyer	(provide legal counsel, litigate)
Grandfather	(protect under older laws and regulations)
Source	(find a vendor or supplier)
Tenure	(grant permanent employment or privileges)

Often it is hard to refrain from these odd and counterfeit coinages; English makes it so easy. Consider the term popularized by TV crime shows: *lawyer-up*. This expression, which means "to exercise one's constitutional right to legal representation," is characteristic of the process. A particular profession needs a word that will replace several, describing a phenomenon that occurs frequently. Applying the rules of verb formation, they invent a good piece of jargon that not only communicates the factual meaning efficiently but even carries with it the tone of irritated contempt that police officers typically feel for the constitutional rights of their *detainees* or *perps*. In communicating with E2s, however, it is better replaced by the longer, less efficient form or, at least, with a convenient glossary entry.

Tactic 19: Be Aware of the Several Englishes

Remember that there is more than one way to spell and punctuate English and that there are even differences in idiom, grammar, and meaning as we travel from one English-speaking country to another. Americans use *company* as a singular, the British as a *plural*. Americans put all commas and periods inside closing quotation marks; the British only some. The verb *to table* has opposite meanings in America (*postpone*) and England (*discuss at once*).

In the UK, *presently* means quite soon, while in North America it means *currently*. In England, one hears *different to,* in America *different from*. (And in all English-speaking nations the form *different than* is substandard.)

North American English:
The Board of Directors has reached no decision.
UK, Chinese, European English:
The Board of Directors have taken no decision.

Again, it is useful to acquire the dictionaries and language guides used in your audiences' countries. Most French or Chinese readers, for example, will have learned English from British teachers and texts; American writers may want to adjust some conventions. In practice, however, an American company that decides to use British conventions ought to engage a British editor to oversee the process. All well-read people are aware of the obvious differences (*color* versus *colour*), but there are scores of subtler differences that elude all but those who are studying them; for example, both *defence* and *defense* exist in British English, with different meanings, and few American readers know this.

Tactic 20: Be Careful with Money and Dates

Be especially clear with shortened forms of dates. In the United States, 5/6/05 means May 6, 2005. Elsewhere in the world, it is more likely to mean June 5.

Note the world's two conflicting conventions for punctuating numbers and money: 1.000.000 versus 1,000,000; $1,212.95 versus $1.212,95. Also note that billion and trillion have different meanings in much of Europe. It is safer to write "3,000 million" than "3 billion." The traditional British interpretation of billion is a million millions—a thousand times what an American means by the word. Recently, however, the American convention has gained many adherents abroad.

Tactic 21: Avoid Illogical or Arbitrary Idioms

An idiom is a sequence of words (two or more) whose meaning cannot be understood from knowledge of the separate words themselves: for example, *put to rest* (formal) or *make short work of* (informal, slang). Typically, there is something arbitrary about an idiom; the expressions might just as easily have been *make to rest* and *put short work of.* Idioms containing prepositions are so arbitrary that they are among the last things language learners acquire. People learning English will often make the idiomatic error *said him.* (The correct idiom is *said to him.*) In English, both *depend on* and *depend from* exist, but not *depend to, depend by, depend with, depend at. Said him* is an error, but not *told him.*

The words *idiom* and *idiomatic* have several meanings, even in the study of grammar. Although most definitions argue that idioms are used and understood by members of a particular community (and puzzling to others), it is nevertheless possible for an educated E1 to make idiomatic errors. For example, though widely used, the expression *comprised of* does not exist in idiomatically correct English.

Generally, teachers of English as a Second Language treat idioms as odd or illogical phrases that are widely known to first language speakers but are mystifying to others. *Pass up, pass by, pass through, pass over, pass along, take a pass . . .* each expression has a meaning unrelated to the words in the phrase, each is unlikely to be defined in any but the largest lexicon, and all should, when possible, be replaced by a single verb whose meaning can be found in the dictionary.

Idiom also refers sometimes to odd figures of speech or even clichés—that is, overworked figures of speech. English is filled with such odd and arbitrary constructions. Even the most austere technical publications contain phrases that, on closer examination, prove to be unnecessarily hard to understand or translate. What, for example, will the E2 reader interpret in the phrase *run a risk?* or *lose ground?* or *bide one's time?*

Moreover, many such expressions are confounding and confusing. In English, for example,

have a few things in common	= is similar to
have few things in common	= is dissimilar from

Interestingly, when I presented this last example to a colleague who teaches English as a Second Language, she assured me that this was precisely the sort of idiomatic problem discussed at length in ESL classes, that I need not alert business and technical writers to avoid the construction. But the notion that clear writing reduces the risk of misunderstanding suggests that, when there is time to edit and there are less difficult alternatives available, the phrases should be replaced.

The reference shelf at most book stores will contain a few collections of English oddities, compiled for our pleasure by writers and editors with an especially sharp ear for the charming vagaries of our language. In these works we see such pairs as

off the books	= not reported (to the tax authorities)
off book	= not reading from a script (theater)

Of course, nearly all languages are filled with these alien idioms. To say one likes something in Modern Hebrew, for example, one says the equivalent of "It puts a charm in my eye." Some Spanish speakers say a thing is lucky by saying it's "a donkey who plays a flute." In French, an influential person has "a long arm." Ironically, just at about the time people learning a language begin to master of few of these odd expressions, someone will come along and tell them that good writers avoid them.

Tactic 22: Avoid Words that Can Have Opposite Meanings

Those compendiums of English oddities usually point out that many English words can have opposite meanings in different contexts—although the context does not always resolve the question of meaning. To computer professionals, for example, *transparent* means invisible, whereas in general business usage it means obvious, especially easy to see. Both of these sentences are idiomatically correct:

- The new security enhancements will be transparent to the agents. (invisible)
- The need for the security enhancements is transparent to the staff. (obvious)

To complicate matters, current political discourse is filled with *transparent* as a synonym for *open,* neither secret nor hidden, accessible to the public. For several reasons, including the fact that it is now fashionable—and good writers, following Orwell's advice, avoid fashionable terms—the word *transparent* should be replaced.

Note these other problematic terms, a small subset of the English words that can mean opposite things at different times:

cleave	to join together or to cut apart
clip	attach or detach
fast	moving or stuck (steadfast)
handicap	disadvantage or advantage
left	still here versus gone
temper	to soften (as in anger) or to harden (as in steel)
screen	to hide from view or to display
scan	to read carefully or to read casually
sanction	to authorize or to punish
oversight	careful review or failure to notice
weather	to withstand pressure, or to wear out

Tactic 23: Avoid Abbreviations, Contractions, and Acronyms

Always dangerous in business or technical communication, shortened forms are especially difficult for E2. Particularly troublesome are references to local agencies and institutions, such as *IRS* or *401(k)*. Of course, some abbreviations—like *IRA*—mean quite different things in different contexts.

Contractions have no place in formal writing, so they should be less of a concern.

> **Before:**
> They'll send a report ASAP.
> **After:**
> They will send a report as soon as possible.

The exception to this tactic is, of course, terms better known in their compressed form than their full form. For example, *IBM* is better known than *International Business Machines*, and few people would recognize a modulator-demodulator as a *modem*.

Note also that a principal drawback to working with charts and diagrams in international documents is that they tend to force writers to use more shortened, telegraphic forms, so as to fit their text, captions, and labels into the cells of their graphics and tables. When possible, one should resize or redraw the graphics so that there is room for unabbreviated headings and labels, including even articles (*the, a, an*) for the nouns. NOTE: Leave even more room if these parts of the graphic are going to be translated.

Tactic 24: Avoid Figurative Language in General

The greatest frustration in conversing with international friends and clients is screening one's language for figures of speech and for words used figuratively. What makes it so difficult is that a natural language is filled with such expressions. Some words—*keen* or *belabor,* for example—have lost their figurative associations and become ordinary prose. To the extent possible, especially in formal writing, E1 authors should sweep their documents for figurative language, replacing as much of it as possible with plainer expressions. Here is a subset of the thousands of expressions:

Instead of . . .	Write
in the first place	first (not firstly)
solo	unassisted
address	discuss
keen	eager/enthusiastic (not "enthused")
sharp	intelligent
hot	popular/fashionable
top drawer	highest quality
cream of the crop	best available choices
gold medal	best
yesterday's news	out of fashion
leading edge	most innovative
cutting edge	too innovative for most
far out	excessive or weird
answer to a prayer	timely solution to a problem
doorbuster	attractively priced

To illustrate, many businesspeople use the term *bail out* to mean *abandon a project,* using the image of a parachutist; sometimes they shorten this just to *bail,* as in *After two bad years, we decided to bail.* At the same time, other business writers use *bail out* to mean *rescue an endangered company,* using the nautical sense of the term; this is the understanding of the expression *government bailout. Bail* also has a technical meaning in the law, as well as in British sports! In short, it is a dangerously confusing term to use in an international document. (Moreover, we will overlook the confusion with *bale.*)

In general, clichés that use figurative language will mystify the reader—unless they have learned their English from watching American TV without subtitles. Proposals and reports probably should be free of such expressions as *between a rock and a hard place* or *slipped through the cracks* or *the more the merrier.* And when such expressions are used, they should be used correctly: for example, *bated breath,* not *baited breath.*

Among the most useful guides for the replacement of figurative and esoteric language is Mary deVries's *Internationally Yours* (1994).

Tactic 25: Avoid Literary and Cultural Allusions

Often in business writing, less often in technical, the language will refer to particular works of literature or other cultural artifacts. Usually, these references are not intellectual or scholarly: rather, they reflect the way in which literature and culture have become embedded in everyday language. Be mindful of

Literary references (note the British spellings to reflect the Shakespearean sources)
• better part of valour
• last refuge of scoundrels
• something is rotten
• heart on his sleeve
• last, best hope
• honoured in the breach

Proverbs and scriptural references
• the last straw
• Lazarus
• pearls before swine
• still, small voice
• move mountains
• under the sun

Popular culture references
• the usual suspects
• two to tango
• an offer he can't refuse
• Disney version
• buy a vowel

It does not matter that "honoured in the breach" and "better part of valour" are from Shakespeare and, therefore, more respectable than other clichés; what matters is that they will more puzzle than enlighten the E2 reader. (I am reminded of the critic who did not like Hamlet because it contained so many clichés.)

Tactic 26: Avoid Military and Sports Vocabulary

Early approaches to the teaching of business and management relied heavily on military science and strategy. That may explain why North American business discourse is overly fond of military terms—most of which translate very badly. Even the book you are reading talks about strategies and tactics. Be wary of such expropriated items as:

• targets
• missions
• objectives
• task forces

- strategies
- intelligence
- chain-of-command
- neutralize
- threat
- theater of operations
- packages
- intervention

In the following example, the revised version is longer but much more likely to be understood.

Before:
Before we target a new market, we need better competitor intelligence.
After:
Before we introduce our product in a new country, we need better information about competitors' products and plans.

Making matters more complicated is the fondness of these same writers for sports imagery, much of which, ironically, derives from military imagery as well. E2 readers will probably be confused by such common North American expressions as

- game plans
- team/team approaches
- full court presses
- going on offense
- keying on the competition
- strike at
- tackle
- blitz
- check
- new set of downs
- huddle with
- goal-line stand
- fourth and long

Sports expressions insinuate themselves into many aspects of our lives. Recently, a visitor from the Middle East told me how puzzled she was by the expression "three strikes and you're out" used in connection with sentencing guides for criminal proceedings!

Tactic 27: Avoid Technical Terms Used with Nontechnical Meanings

Modern business communication requires writers and readers to know a considerable computer and systems vocabulary. For example, it is extremely useful to know what a *module* is, what an *interface* does, and whether information will be processed in a *batch* or in *real-time*. But it is not useful, especially to people who are already struggling with ambiguous sports and military terminology, to use computer and systems expressions for the description of ordinary business events. Generally, technological vocabulary should be reserved for writing about technology. When terms such as *interface* slip into general business documents, they can be very hard to interpret or translate.

Instead of . . .	Write
system	tool, device
integrate	add, mix, introduce
initialize	begin
interface with	meet, call
positive feedback	favorable response
database	files
generation	type, style, version
multimedia	video or movie
capability	ability, power, feature
platform	machine, method
environment	setting
multi-tasking	being too busy

Environment is often a superfluous word. *A banking environment* is usually a *bank; experience in a UNIX environment* is usually *UNIX experience.*

The habit of adding high-tech words to ordinary discourse grows from that most suspect of writer's impulses: the attempt to make the ordinary sound difficult and impressive. By this reasoning, people who *interface* should receive more money than people who merely talk on the phone and people with *experience in a multi-platform environment* are more desirable than people who can use both Linux and Windows.

When writers use these terms, even in a nontechnical context, they should at least be sure to use them correctly. For example, every day thousands of politicians, curriculum coordinators, and such use *positive feedback* to mean favorable response to an event or proposal. In fact, positive feedback—amplification of deviations—is the process that causes the unbearable screech to emanate from loudspeakers. In Economics it is the process that makes the rich richer and poor poorer.

Similarly, *module* is used to describe everything from chapters in textbooks to lawn chairs. In the process, modularity, one of the more beautiful and elusive constructs in engineering, is reduced to a shallow buzzword, all because of an attempt to make something as pedestrian as a classroom exercise sound like high-technology.

Tactic 28: Avoid Business Jargon and Fashionable Business Terms

The trouble with fashionable words and phrases is that, like all fashions, they quickly become unfashionable. Used in speaking, they are harmless enough; as the fashions change we can adjust our vocabularies. But writing is persistent; manuals, reports, plans, and proposals can have an effective life of several years. Moreover, the documents in a company's files tend to be copied and reused in later documents. A brief description of a project can reappear in a company's proposals and plans for decades. This reused material is called *boilerplate,* another figurative expression that will confuse the E2 reader.

The second problem with fashionable language is that, as people become eager to use it, they are less precise about its meaning. For example, when everyone was interested in quality in the mid-1990s, the word was used so often in so many contexts that business scholars began publishing papers containing elaborate conceptual frameworks— just to explicate the numerous meanings of the term. The meaning became so imprecise and diffused that, to a large extent, any sentence containing *quality* could be interpreted in a half dozen ways, all defensible; in effect, it was no longer possible to do business research with *quality* as an understandable variable. In the past five years, *globalization* has begun to manifest the same pattern, meaning very different things to different supporters and opponents.

Businesspeople are especially susceptible to management fads and the vocabularies associated with them. Management consultants often give new names to old constructs—*structured analysis* becomes *reengineering,* for example—creating the illusion of new knowledge. In messages for international readers, however, these fashionable expressions can be treacherous. Unless these terms are defined in a glossary, international documents should be free of buzzwords—overworked words, or any words uniquely associated with a particular management theory or popular management consultant. Among the hundreds of risky terms are

- reengineer (or re-engineer)
- quality, total quality
- empowerment
- prioritize
- impact, impactful
- downsize, right-size
- self-actualization
- globalization
- synergy
- enterprise solution
- information architecture
- knowledge management
- downside, upside

Visit the entertaining *Word Spy* website (http://www.wordspy.com/index/Business-Buzzwords.asp) to see whether you recognize the most current buzzwords. But don't use the words you find there in your international communications.

When one of these terms is correct and necessary, the writer's obligation is to define and explain it in the text AND in a glossary. Generally, however, a word like *downside* can be replaced with such ordinary terms as *risk, loss, problem,* or *disadvantage.* The noun *impact* can mean *effect, result, damage, change, loss, consequence* (I have asked people who perform Environmental Impact Studies what *impact* means; about half say it means *effect* and about half say *negative effect*). *Impact* as a verb has no place in writing, except for those who are discussing asteroids and wisdom teeth.

Tactic 29: Avoid Regionalisms and Slang

Obviously, globalizing one's English means removing much of its flavor and fun; the very expressions that make prose familiar, endearing, and warm are those likely to be wrapped in cultural and literary references, or embedded in figurative language. Well-educated or, at least, well-read E1s find it hard to write an interesting sentence without some element that requires the reader to have cultural sensitivity or background in English-speaking culture. For each of these thousands of small cultural problems of English in general, there may be several more regional variations, including slang and casual expressions, that work their way into business and professional communication.

Aside from the obviously inappropriate regional slang expression, (like *that dog won't hunt*), there are also subtler regionalisms that crop up (like *crop up*) in business documents. For example, certain regions of the United States and UK use the verb *reckon* to mean assess or appraise; in the United States it is regional slang, whereas in the UK it is the Queen's English; it will translate poorly. Writers from New York often use the expression *kind of* for *somewhat*. British and Canadian writers will begin sentences with *mind you,* where Americans prefer *of course*. Americans will overuse *basically* in much the way that British E1s overuse *actually:* as far as I can tell, neither word means anything at all. *Basically* and *actually* are useful to extemporaneous speakers who do not want to say *um* or *uh;* they should be cut from most written sentences.

Regions can also confuse and conflate idioms. Most people pronounce *cater-corner* as *catty-corner,* which becomes *kitty-corner* in some places. Many Americans, for example, fuse *gerrymander* (a political term that refers to the corrupt drawing of political boundaries) with *jury rig* (a nautical term that describes a quick, temporary solution) and say *gerry-rig*.

Tactic 30: Avoid Sarcasm or Irony

Irony and its coarser cousins, sarcasm and wisecrack, can be baffling; they usually fail in formal writing, especially for audiences culturally removed from the writer. Without a shared culture of vocal inflections, and without use of the voice, there is little chance that the meaning of the passages will be taken correctly.

For people raised in certain parts of the world, however, irony and sarcasm are daily habits of speech, so deeply ingrained that speakers are unaware of their use and often seem incapable of expressing judgments without them. For example, I was once engaged to help a branch of the

U.S. Army improve some of its documentation. In a memo, I made the mistake of writing: "There is no documentation at all for the base telephone system. None. Fortunately, it's not used for any important messages." And my reader took me literally, perplexed that I could reach such an unwarranted conclusion.

Amusingly, many writers believe they can accomplish the full range of inflections and suprasegmental phonemes (pitch, stress, and intonation) required to deliver a snide remark by inserting a few strategic quotation marks. But sneering with quotation marks does not translate either: We read your "long-range plan." (What you disingenuously refer to as your long-range plan.) If you have an editorial comment, do it with words (*so-called* or *alleged* plan) rather than trying to do it with quotation marks. And no speaker should ever express skepticism by making a hand gesture resembling quotation marks.

Because of the international variations in the conventions for quotation marks, I urge writers to use them only when necessary, and certainly not to suggest an ironic or skeptical tone.

Tactic 31: Avoid Humor and Wordplay

So far, writers of International English have been urged against jargon, slang, odd idioms, literary allusions, and nearly all forms of figurative language. As I have emphasized, nearly all forms of wordplay, verbal cleverness, or puns will distract or mislead the international reader. Although formal manuals, proposals, or reports usually contain relatively little of such material, it often finds its way into correspondence, e-mail, and other short messages.

Possibly the most dangerous practice of all is taking an already obscure cliché or literary reference and altering it for humorous effect: *between a rock and a lawsuit, skipped through the cracks, the more the messier.* At the very least, if we expect E2s to understand clichés and literary references, we ought to leave them intact. Many writers lose any chance of communicating by upsetting the internal logic of the clichés themselves. If you wish to express indifference, write: *I couldn't care less* (not *I could care less*, which makes no sense.) Moreover, the correct formation is: You cannot eat your cake and have it too. (There is nothing difficult about having a cake, then eating it.)

As to humor, although there may be relatively little humor in business and technical writing, occasionally one sees a kind of wisecracking in, for example, software screen messages. Also, experience suggests that the casual mood associated with e-mail communication—the tolerance for informal style and freewheeling grammar and syntax—encourages people to write in a more speech-like manner, with a nearly inevitable lapse into wordplay and slang.

Remember that humor is the material most resistant to interpretation or translation and that, unless it is genuinely important to the message, it should be pared away.

Tactic 32: Suit Your English Idiom to the Local Language

The tactics thus far recommended in this chapter are part of the globalization, or culture-free, approach to International English. The objective in every case is to remove from the latest draft of the document those phrases and constructions that are familiar to an advanced speaker of English but that probably have not been taught to E2 readers with only a few months or years of English education.

As mentioned in the introduction, culture-free, one-size-fits-all English is usually the most efficient way to speak to a large, heterogeneous audience of E2s. In contrast, there are times when our English materials are intended for E2s in a small number of specific countries. In these cases, it might make good business sense to produce more than one English version, sensitive to the first language of the readers.

Often English gives us a choice of idioms and, therefore, the option to choose an idiom that is close to the idiomatic structure of E2's first language. For example, suppose the original text in a software manual read:

> There is a way to save several passages at once to the Clipboard.

An E2 whose first language is German would probably prefer:

> One can save several passages at once in the Clipboard. (like the German *man* construction)

In contrast, an E2 whose first language is Hebrew might prefer:

> It is possible to save several passages at once in the Clipboard. (like the Hebrew *efshar* construction)

It seems excessively hard to apply this principle to long documents for several audiences; among other things it requires editors who know both languages. But the application in which it makes most sense is a document containing instructions, in which the same sentence pattern may occur scores of times. Just as most American readers would be irritated by an instruction manual written entirely in the third person *(The customer should type his or her Personal Identification Number.)*, so might a German reader, already taxed by the use of English, resent page after page of the typically American imperative format *(Type your Personal Identification Number.)*.

Again, the issue is a business question: Would it help a company to win and support customers to have specialized English versions? Would it provide a competitive advantage? Would the expected return exceed the marginal cost?

There are, of course, many American writers who think that the second version of the instruction *(Type your Personal Identification Number.)* is inherently better in all circumstances—leaner, clearer, easier to read—and should never be replaced with the wordy third-person version. For them the issue is more culturally complicated: Should the goal of adapting to the cultural and language preferences of readers ever take precedence over certain universal principles of clear, readable writing? Principles that are central to their profession? We reserve this question for a later chapter.

Discussion Questions

- Have you endured expense or bad feelings as the sender of an unclear message?
- Have you ever lost time or money trying to follow unclear instructions?
- Do you regularly use any military or sports imagery in your business or professional discussions?
- Do you find it reasonable and practicable to compose and edit your e-mails on a word processor before you send them?
- Have you encountered a theory of business or management in which you suspected that the ideas were old and the vocabulary new?
- Can you describe a business or professional situation from your experience in which humor or sarcasm led to a misunderstanding?

Sources and Resources

Axtell, Roger. *Do's and Taboos of Using English around the World*. New York: John Wiley & Sons, 1995.

deVries, Mary. *Internationally Yours: Writing and Communicating Successfully in Today's Global Marketplace*. Boston: Houghton-Mifflin, 1994.

Flesch, Rudolf. *How to Write Plain English: A Book for Lawyers and Consumers*. New York: Harper and Row, 1979.

Lanham, Richard. *Revising Business Prose*. 3rd ed. New York: Macmillan Publishing, 1992.

Lanham, Richard. *Style: An Anti-Textbook*. New Haven, CT: Yale University Press, 1974.

Moss, Norman. *British/American Language Dictionary*. Lincolnwood, IL: Passport Books, 1984.

Neiditz, Minerva. *Business Writing at Its Best*. Burr Ridge, IL: Irwin Professional Publishing, 1994.

Owl Online Writing Lab, Purdue University (http://owl.english.purdue.edu/internet/resources/genre.html)

Pinker, Steven. *Words and Rules*. New York: Basic Books, 1999.

Williams, Joseph. *Style: Ten Lessons in Clarity and Grace*. 6th ed. Chicago: University of Chicago Press, 2000.

Zinsser, William. *On Writing Well*, 25th Anniversary Edition. New York: HarperResource, 2001.

4

Reducing Burdens

Reading is stressful. It burdens not only the mind but the eyes, sometimes even the hands. Each reader, E1 or E2, approaches a document with an expectation of the effort or exertion needed to process the material on that page or screen. When that level is exceeded, the reader reduces the effort by reading less carefully: skimming, glossing, or skipping. When even those adjustments cannot bring the reading effort to a reasonable level, the reader abandons the document in frustration. The objective of this chapter, therefore, is to identify the commonplace practices that unnecessarily burden all readers, especially E2s.

Reading and Stress

Anyone who has tried to study when tired knows what the researchers have found about reading: it is hard work, requiring energy, focus, and alertness. Tired readers absorb little, unable to remember anything from the last several pages. Indeed, many people put themselves to sleep by reading; the more demanding the document, the swifter the effect. Readability, the index of how difficult a text is to read, measures not just the intellectual effort required to decipher and interpret the sentences; it also measures the sheer, raw energy needed to stay focused and process the symbols into meaning.

Outside the world of avant-garde literature, increasing the burden on a reader produces predictably bad results. Recommendations are misunderstood; instructions are followed incorrectly; sales propositions are unappreciated. When a document presses the limits of a reader's powers, the result is a perfunctorily skimmed message at best, an ignored unread message at worst.

This is true for all readers at all times. That is why nearly every principle of editing style, in nearly every book and article on the subject, has the same objective: to reduce the exertion required of the readers. Thus, the active voice, unpretentious vocabulary, and even the appropriate use of punctuation are all important for readability. Most people can become better writers or editors merely by reflecting on all the things they dislike in the publications they are obliged to read or use and by taking steps to eliminate those things from their own writing. For example, almost no reader likes small print, narrow margins, long sentences and paragraphs, an absence of headings and summaries, or pompous vocabulary. All we have to do to improve our writing is promise not to burden our own readers with the very practices that tire and frustrate us.

Reading a language other than one's main language is inherently tiring. E2s with more advanced skills will find it less stressful than those with limited language training. But what readers would not be more exhausted by a half hour with their second language than their first! It follows then that, much as it is important to enhance the readability of all writing, it is critical to International English Style.

The benefits of short words and sentences are even greater in international communication than in messages between E1s, though there are exceptions. In International English, *conclude* might be better than *hold,* and the longer phrase *topic that arouses a strong response* is probably better than the shorter *hot button.* But these exceptions notwithstanding, writing for E2 demands even shorter words and simpler sentences than other kinds of English. It is nearly inconceivable that an idiomatic first draft, written by an author accustomed to communicating with other E1 colleagues, will produce material that is suitable for E2 readers. It is also unlikely that one cursory pass through the text—what passes for editing in most companies—will produce the necessary results. Editing for E2 takes a while—and phrases like *takes a while* need to be replaced.

Tactic 33: Prefer Shorter Sentences

There are two main ways to shorten a first draft sentence: first, to replace wordy constructions with simpler ones; second, to break complex and compound sentences into two or more sentences. By applying methods already explained, the following sentence loses some of its excess weight:

> **Before:**
> We make no specific guarantees with respect to future rate of return on these investment instruments.
> **After:**
> We guarantee no specific return on these funds.

In the next example, a single sentence is divided into its simpler components:

> **Before:**
> Should your estimated prepayments result in an excess balance in your account, be advised that you have the option to choose between a credit and refund.
> **After:**
> Sometimes, your estimated payments equal more than you owe. Do you have a balance in your account? If so, we can either send you a refund or give you a credit. OR

> • Estimated payments sometimes equal more than you owe.
> • Do you have a balance in your account?
> • If so, we can either
>   • send you a refund or
>   • give you a credit

These improvements would be helpful not only to E2 readers but to E1 readers as well. When sentences contain procedural or technical information, it is nearly impossible to make them too simple. This is not true, however, when sentences contain *concepts* (ideas, conclusions, or analyses). Because sentences edited this way, of necessity, will be shorter, a document for an E2 audience will almost certainly sound choppy and a bit unsophisticated to E1 readers. The style may seem a bit clipped because there will be much less subordination and, therefore, much more repetition of essential nouns. Nearly all sentences will begin with the subject. It will often resemble the dull, primer writing style of typical undergraduates.

As powerful, then, as sentences starting with *because* or *although* may be in most conceptual writing, relatively few of them should appear in international documents. By traditional standards, a well-written International English document, lacking the complex sentences associated with mature discussion, seems underwritten or juvenile. Consider this sample:

Before:
Unless these terms are defined in a glossary, international documents should be free of "buzzwords," overworked words, or any words uniquely associated with a particular management theory or fashionable management consultant.

After:
In international documents, do not use overworked or fashionable words. Avoid words that are part of a particular management theory; also avoid words made popular by a particular management consultant. If you must use these words, however, define them in a glossary.

Not all conceptual writing will be injured by the application of International English Style, but it is clear that much of it will be less appropriate for E1 readers than simple factual or instructional materials, the kind found in manuals and instructions. In other words, good technical writing (except perhaps for the Introduction and Discussion section of scientific papers) is already closer in editorial discipline to International English than, say, marketing communication.

Interestingly, if the conceptual material is mostly empty verbiage, with few specific claims or straightforward arguments, then trying to edit it for an E2 reader will expose its emptiness and reveal its dishonesty. Honest product advertising that describes actual features and benefits of products can be reliably edited for an E2 reader. Oblique and suggestive brand advertising, however, with its soft associations and lack of product information, resists attempts to render it more clearly and simply.

Tactic 34: Prefer Simple Sentences to Compound Sentences

As numerous tactics in this text illustrate, the most straightforward way to shorten sentences is to reduce wordy phrases and clauses to single words and short clauses. Thus, the phrase *it appears that* becomes *apparently* and *make a choice of* becomes *choose*. The next best way is to break apart compound sentences—those connected with semicolons or coordinating conjunctions (*and, or, but*) into two or more sentences.

> **Before:**
> The sentences will be shorter; there will be much less subordination and, therefore, much more repetition of essential nouns; nearly all sentences will begin with the subject.
> **After:**
> The sentences will be shorter. The sentences will contain much less subordination. Therefore, there will be much more repetition of essential nouns. Nearly all sentences will begin with the subject.

> **Before:**
> Usually, these references are not intellectual or scholarly: rather, they reflect the way in which literature and culture become embedded in everyday language.
> **After:**
> Usually, these references are not intellectual or scholarly. Rather, they reflect how literature and culture are embedded in everyday language.

Not surprisingly, eliminating some of these basic efficiencies of syntax sometimes results in longer passages, with more words repeated to accomplish the same task. But most of the sentences are shorter and therefore, less daunting to E2.

Tactic 35: Prefer Simple Sentences to Complex Sentences

Unfortunately, complex and complex-compound sentences are far more difficult to understand than simple and compound sentences. I say "unfortunately" because, as hard as it is to write an engaging analysis, conclusion, or recommendation without figurative language and idioms, it is even more difficult to write genuinely thoughtful or interesting passages without an occasional complex sentence. Those teachers and consultants who overemphasize the value of short, simple sentences (possibly because they do not trust their students and clients to write longer ones) have not reached the conclusion that Jacques Barzun reached long ago in his classic *Simple and Direct* (1985): namely, that the sentences richest in meaning and content, the sentences that distill and conclude, are complex sentences. This is, in my experience, the most regrettable difference between clear standard English and International English: the deconstruction of tight, thoughtful complex sentences into loosely connected simple sentences.

> **Before:**
> I say "unfortunately" because, as hard as it is to write an engaging analysis, conclusion, or recommendation without figurative language and idioms, it is even more difficult to write genuinely thoughtful or interesting passages without an occasional complex sentence.
>
> **After:**
> I call this rule unfortunate. Why? It is hard enough to write an engaging analysis, conclusion, or recommendation without figurative language and idioms. It is even harder to write genuinely thoughtful or interesting passages without an occasional complex sentence.

Tactic 36: Retain Certain Optional Words

Removing unnecessary words is among the first few tactics in any list of style rules, especially those aimed at International English. But it is dangerous to be overzealous in cutting words. Sometimes it is more helpful to the reader to retain a few of those otherwise removable words. Certain optional words in English make the logic of a sentence much clearer. International readers will have an easier time with sentences that include these extra words. The most recurring example is the *that* appearing before indirect speech:

> **Before:**
> We do not believe the management will forget its promises.
> **After:**
> We do not believe *that* the management will forget its promises.

The flaw in the Before sentence is that it misleads the readers, who see *We do not believe the management* before they realize that the sentence means the opposite.

Usually, sentences should be truthful from the beginning, reading from left to right, and should not contain late material that amends an earlier claim. When the sentence logic forces the reader to double back, this is an example of a *GOTO*, a reverse of direction that adds to the reader's burden.

Similarly, in international documents, it is usually safer to repeat nouns than to point at them with pronouns such as *this, these, which,* or *who; this X* or *that Y* is preferable. Unclear relative and personal pronouns, such as *he* or *they,* should be replaced with repeated nouns.

> **Before:**
> We have assessed the improvements to the accounting tools, which, in our opinion, do not justify the cost of the upgrade. (What does the word *which* refer to?)
> **After:**
> We have assessed the improvements to the accounting tools. These few improvements, in our opinion, do not justify the cost of the upgrade.

It is also useful to repeat words that are sometimes omitted in pairs, as in:

> **Before:**
> The team will be ready to start work and write the first report by December 1.
> **After:**
> The team will be ready to start work and *to* write the first report by December 1.

Even when the goal is to waste no words, it is still dangerous to write in *telegraphic* style, so named because it refers to the day when people sending telegrams would be charged by the word and would edit accordingly.

Punctuation and International English

Some punctuation marks, such as the full stop period, are required; others, like the comma after such introductory phrases as *of course,* are helpful, though optional. A good many of the punctuation marks in American business documents are neither—for example, the embarrassing apostrophe in the possessive *its.*

After years of editing American reports and papers, I have concluded that most American college graduates who are not professional writers or teachers know very few of the rules of punctuation. Many would make the error, for example, of setting off the restrictive clause—*who are not professional writers or teachers*—with commas. Their commas and apostrophes appear almost at random; they confuse hyphens and dashes—and almost never use dashes; they rarely set off nonrestrictive clauses with commas because, indeed, most have no idea what a clause is, let alone a nonrestrictive one. In fact, a substantial minority of the educated adults I meet claim that they were never taught grammar and punctuation in school at all!

Making matters worse, the replacement of most kinds of short business correspondence with e-mail has exacerbated the problem, giving most business writers the sense that punctuation and spelling and grammar are of minor consequence in business communication. This last trend is most regrettable; as I shall argue in Chapter 6, *every badly written, underedited, ill-formed word and sentence in an e-mail injures the sender.* And even though the sender may have saved time by not reviewing and revising the document, nothing could do more to help the sender's career than to make the needed improvements in his or her document.

The absence or randomness of punctuation in most business writing is understandable among people who have never been convinced that grammar and style could possibly affect their professional goals. But American English, and even British English to an extent, is also influenced by the journalistic indifference toward refinements of punctuation, especially commas. Generally, American newspaper writers would not have put the comma after the *generally* at the beginning of this sentence. Nor do they put commas before the *and* or *or* in a series. Inherent in this practice is, on the one hand, a preference for fast, muscular prose that moves without pauses or detours and, on the other, contempt for layered, parenthetical constructions within sentences. Journalists, like nearly everyone, dislike academic and scholarly prose, and they take pains to avoid constructions and styles that smack of it.

The point that every writer must appreciate, especially those brave enough to communicate with E2, is that sentences, once they extend beyond five or six words, *need punctuation to be understood.* Punctuation is neither a cosmetic decoration nor an affectation of style—and certainly not a game played to satisfy one's school teachers. It is the technique that tells us which words in a sentence are related to which, what modifies what, and how the logic of the utterance is to be processed. Louis Menand made this point well in a recent magazine piece:

> The function of most punctuation—commas, colons and semicolons, dashes, and so on—is to help organize the relationships among the parts of a sentence. Its role is semantic: to add precision and complexity to meaning. It increases the information potential of strings of words. (2004, p. 103)

Menand might also have mentioned that punctuation *increases* information by *decreasing* the number of potential misreadings, thereby taking away some guesswork. Just as a well-designed mechanical device discourages operators from using it inappropriately, a well-punctuated sentence makes itself harder to misunderstand. To illustrate, just recently I read a British article containing the following sentence: *By the time it ended the effects of the war were devastating.* The lack of a comma after *ended* is more than a small stylistic failure to set off an introductory phrase; it also encourages a misreading of the sentence, causing many to inadvertently construct the unintended *ended the effects* and forcing them to reread the passage.

Most journalists, however, take the fully defensible position that a well-built sentence should be clear and unambiguous with little or no punctuation. By keeping sentences short-and-simple, they say, and using reliable syntax, you should not need dashes and parentheses to make a point. This attitude, with its emphasis on simplicity and directness of form, is entirely appropriate for International English Style. E2 readers will generally prefer two independent sentences with full stops to a pair of independent clauses linked by a semicolon. Most E2s would prefer that a parenthetical apposition—that is, an explanation of the previous phrase set off in commas, parentheses, or dashes—appear in the next sentence, instead of being intruded into the flow of the first sentence. Consider the difference:

Before:
> Most E2s would prefer a parenthetical apposition (that is, an explanation of the previous phrase set off in commas, parentheses, or dashes) to appear in the next sentence, instead of being intruded into the flow of the first sentence.

After:
> Most E2s would prefer a parenthetical apposition to appear in the next sentence, instead of being intruded into the flow of the first sentence. (An apposition is an explanation of the previous phrase set off in commas, parentheses, or dashes.)

Writers of International English, then, are obliged to learn and remember the punctuation rules for their own nation's English and, then, must be prepared to modify and revise those rules on the few occasions when it will help to reduce the burden on the reader or discourage misreading. Moreover, if they work in settings where professional editors review their writing, they should be prepared for a conflict or two. Editors, whose authority is often limited by soft and hard-to-explain principles of style, cling fast to unambiguous punctuation rules and may blanch at the thought of breaking one on purpose.

Tactic 37: Use Commas Aggressively

Professional writers often disagree about the use of punctuation, especially the comma. Most journalists use as few as possible, but some academic writers insert one in nearly every pause. In most cases, this second approach will be more helpful to E2, enabling the reader to divide the sentence into its components and more easily follow its logic.

Before:
> In the 90s video artists chose their technology from among Windows based computers, Macintosh or the proprietary and hard to support Amiga computer.

After:
> In the 90s, video artists chose their technology from Windows based computers, Macintosh, or the proprietary—and hard to support—Amiga computer.

Note also the use of em-dashes to set off *and hard to support*. Although commas might be used here, they might also mislead the E2 reader into thinking there is another item in the series. Dashes and parentheses within a sentence are most useful in texts where the commas are being used simultaneously for some other purpose, like a series.

In International English, it is always helpful to set off introductory phrases and to put a coma before the *and, or,* or *nor* in a series.

Before:
> As usual the Canadian, Mexican and Guatemalan subcommittees were the first to report.

After:
> As usual, the Canadian, Mexican, and Guatemalan subcommittees were the first to report.

The most dangerous, potentially confusing commas are those used for two purposes at once: for example, to separate items in a list and the words within the items. A string like *London, Ontario, Yonkers, New York and New York, New York* will baffle most readers, especially those who are unfamiliar with the geography; it should be *London, Ontario; Yonkers, New York; and New York, New York.* Or, better still:

- London, Ontario
- Yonkers, New York
- New York, New York

Tactic 38: Use Hyphens Aggressively

Guiding most of the advice given in this text is consideration for readers who may have to consult a bilingual dictionary—a task familiar to nearly every educated adult. Bilingual dictionaries are often exceedingly difficult to use, especially if they are organized according to an unfamiliar alphabet. One of the most frustrating things about them is that, like all dictionaries, they do not list every word that can be formed with prefixes. They do not include suffixes either, but since the first letter of a word is so critical in looking it up, that is not a massive problem. For example, *The American Heritage Dictionary of the English Language,* 4th ed., contains thirteen pages of words beginning with the letters *pre,* including *preamp, prenuptial, pretreat,* and *pretest,* without hyphens. None of those words are likely to appear in the average bilingual dictionary; indeed, *pretreat* is not recognized by the Microsoft Word thesaurus or spell-checker. Furthermore, almost no English dictionary and no bilingual dictionary will list *preprint* or *prewarm.*

Most writers of English use too many hyphens, inserting them unnecessarily into words like *prerequisite, semicolon, antibiotic.* In writing for E2, however, it is better to err on the side of too many hyphens, especially when they are used to separate prefixes from stems. In this way, even though there is an error of punctuation, the E2 reader will have a better chance of deducing the meaning of the word or, at least, looking it up. At the very least, we should hyphenate words that were routinely hyphenated until the current generation: *co-operate, pre-eminent, co-author.*

Before:
> As usual, the Canadian, Mexican, and Guatemalan subcommittees were the first to report.

After:
> As usual, the Canadian, Mexican, and Guatemalan sub-committees were the first to report.

It is also helpful to link unit and compound modifiers and nouns. Ordinarily, English hyphenates compound and unit modifiers that appear before the noun, but not after. Both sentences below are correct:

> Only research-based proposals were allowed into the discussion.

> We allowed into the discussion only proposals that were research based.

For E2's benefit, both instances should be hyphenated.

Before:
> In the 90s, video artists chose their technology from Windows based computers, Macintosh, or the proprietary—and hard to support—Amiga computer.

After:
> In the 90s, video artists chose their technology from Windows-based computers, Macintosh, or the proprietary—and hard-to-support—Amiga computer.

In writing for anyone, especially E2, we should be on the alert for words that are impossible to pronounce (like *deice* versus *de-ice*) or that might be misread without a hyphen:

- resent vs. re-sent
- refuse vs. re-fuse

Refuse is another example of a word with so many possible misreadings that it is best avoided in International English.

Tactic 39: Avoid Quotation Marks

Possibly the most distracting punctuation is the quotation mark. Although many EIs scatter their apostrophes and commas somewhat randomly, there is nothing random about the consistent misuse of quotation marks, more specifically the other punctuation marks adjacent to them. Exacerbating the problem is the fact that British and American standards for quotation marks are different; most other languages using quotation marks follow the British convention, not the American, and, to be candid, the American convention is illogical.

The American and Canadian rule for punctuation near quotation marks, contrary to all logic, is as follows: *Periods and commas ALWAYS go inside quotation marks, whether or not they logically belong there.* This is known as the *closed convention*, which contrasts with the *logical convention* of putting the periods and commas either inside or outside, depending on the meaning or context. Americans also use the logical convention in connection with parentheses, further confusing the issue. Nonetheless, many, possibly most, Americans regularly violate the closed convention. They will nearly always choose the logical model:

> **Logical (UK):**
> After your "sabbatical", we expect you to work extra hard.
> I have no faith in what he calls his "best estimate".
> **Closed (USA):**
> After your "sabbatical," we expect you to work extra hard.
> I have no faith in what he calls his "best estimate."

The closed convention is so illogical that William Safire, a major newspaper columnist—who is also an expert on English style—claims that he submits his columns using the logical convention, as a protest, and forces the copy editor to make the changes. Moreover, when I explain the rule in classes and seminars, or when I correct the error in the documents of a corporate client, I often encounter outright resistance or rebellion, an insistence that the rule I am teaching does not exist or, more often, that it violates the rule taught by a beloved school teacher. Many school teachers, including more than a few English teachers, do not know this rule. (These may be the same teachers who tell their students that there is a rule against starting an English sentence with the word *because*.)

No academy or institution makes the laws of English, but here are the requirements set forth by two well-known style authorities:

- 8.144. The comma and the final period will be placed inside the quotation marks. (United States Government Printing Office *Style Manual*)
- Place commas and periods within closing quotation marks, whether or not they were included in the original material. (*The Canadian Style,* The Department of the Secretary of State of Canada)

Confusing the matter further is the American convention that requires the placement of all colons and semicolons OUTSIDE the quotation marks, regardless of context or meaning.

Before:
The prize for the best article went to "Revisiting the Whorf-Sapir Hypothesis;" it was the only paper submitted.
After:
The prize for the best article went to "Revisiting the Whorf-Sapir Hypothesis"; it was the only paper submitted.

In North American English, the only punctuation marks that may be used logically—appearing either inside or outside—are question marks, exclamation points, and dashes. All the following sentences are correct:

- His speech was called, "Who Benefits from Currency Exchange?"
- Are you the one who described him as "unmotivated"?
- He actually called us "members of a Western conspiracy"!
- "Yes," he said, "Leibniz & Frege Associates are members of a Western conspiracy!"

The Microsoft Word Style Checker is also confused about this intercontinental punctuation debate. It has set up alternatives that allow you to require the punctuation to be either inside or outside the quotation marks, or not checked at all.

Punctuation should rarely call attention to itself. Unless the writer is using language in some strange or artificial way, the punctuation should be helpful and enabling without distracting from the text. It follows, then, that quotation marks are a continuing and rather intractable problem in International English. Writers are never sure what convention to use; even when they use the right convention it seems illogical. A substantial number of readers may notice or be distracted by the convention, whether or not it is used correctly. The only sensible course, then, is to limit, or even eliminate, quotation marks from International English—perhaps from business writing in general.

This recommendation is more practicable than it seems at first. From the beginnings of writing, there have been major languages that function without either the quotation mark or an analogous convention. Moreover, many of the quotation marks in contemporary business communications are not used for quotations at all, but, rather, to highlight or characterize a string of words. Some journals put the names of articles and papers in quotation marks; others do not. Some writers use quotation marks to set off strings of computer code; others use them to express sarcasm (a very poor technique for International English). In fact, many of the uses of quotation marks in business writing appear to be a throwback to the typewriter era, when there were so few ways to highlight or emphasize text. Before the electronic typewriter, the only way to highlight a string of characters was to use capital letters, the underscore, or quotation marks. Today's business writers are astonished to learn that as recently as the 1980s, boldface and italics required the writer to remove and replace the physical typing element.

The better path, however, is to use other conventions for highlighting: alternate typefaces or fonts, boldface, italics, shading, or color. Such devices must be used consistently and with restraint, but they have the power to eliminate most quotation marks and, thereby, to eliminate a continuing distraction from international documents.

The Burdensome Page

The most dramatic way to reduce the burden on any reader, especially E2s, is to reconsider how words are distributed on a page. Traditionally, the guiding principle for printing text has been governed by the need to conserve paper. Unfortunately, however, nearly every printing standard that conserves paper reduces readability. No one whose job entails a lot of reading appreciates wide columns, small print, long paragraphs, or lack of headings and illustrations. No one who needs to consult Figure 1 wants to go searching for it; no one wants to use two manuals or publications to perform a single task. Such unqualified generalizations are rare in discussing communication principles, but they are safe in this case.

The presentation of text on the page is never a question of cosmetics or of prettying up the document. Page layout and design directly affect the speed, ease, and reliability with which a page will be read. Document design and organization directly affect the number of people who will read and use a publication successfully, and their subsequent attitude toward the people who imposed the material upon them. It is widely believed that some technical documents, including software manuals, will be read by nearly no one, regardless of how well they are written and designed. Perhaps it is more accurate to say that the well-made manuals at least have a chance.

Designing a page well may be likened to giving a gift to the E2 readers, who already are being coerced into working in their second language. Narrowing a column, converting a paragraph to a bullet list, putting glossary terms at the bottom of each page—these and other practices increase the probability that the reader's task will be lightened enough so that the document is likely to read.

Tactic 40: Do not Justify Text, but Do not Break Words at the Ends of Lines

In printing parlance, *justified text* is text that is flush or straight on both sides. A column that is not justified is said be *ragged*. Technically, there is no such thing as "right justification" or "left justification"; the correct terms are flush-left, ragged-right and flush-right, ragged-left.

Justification is an ancient and revered calligraphic art. The earliest biblical scribes, by making minute adjustments in the spacing ("kerning") of letters and changes in the widths of certain letters, were able to produce precisely justified, correction- and error-free pages with a pen. The more celebrated scribes were even able to adjust the spaces between lines ("leading") so that the first letter on each page would spell out a secret acrostic, sometimes the name of the anonymous scribe.

The point of this digression is to demonstrate that text justification has been deeply revered over the centuries. This veneration intensified as printing technology replaced the work of the scribe. By the seventeenth century, the only way an author could see his or her work justified was to see it in print, that is, published. This situation conferred an additional significance on justification. Writers, scholars, academics, scientists—all those whose goal was publication—would have visible evidence of their success the day the justified galley proofs arrived in the mail.

Word processing machines, followed by software, changed all that. Until recently, every ordinary letter and memo was justified. Today, fortunately, Microsoft Word defaults to flush-left, ragged-right. Now that it is so easy to justify and now that any document can have the look of a published work, it is often difficult to convince people generally that justified paragraphs, ·especially long justified paragraphs, are uninviting to the reader and that in most tests of document usability, the justified paragraphs are more likely to be skimmed or misread than flush-left, ragged-right. (For the best study of the effect of page layout, see Schriver, 1997.)

In general, then, writers of International English should refrain from justifying the text and use a ragged-right text, without hyphens. Despite the somewhat unfamiliar appearance of such pages, they will be much easier to interpret and translate.

Also, it is best to turn off the automatic hyphenation in your system. The recommendation given earlier to use hyphens aggressively does not extend to breaking words at the ends of lines. Hyphenation is a bizarre practice that inconveniences all readers and may utterly thwart the objectives of E2.

Before:

> According to the Memorandum of Understanding between BLM and ADC, BLM is responsible for preparing environmental documents pursuant to the National Environmental Policy Act (NEPA). Adequate documents have not been completed for all BLM districts, and some appeals were filed by environmental organizations. On April 6,1993, BLM instructed their State Directors to have APHIS cease ADC activities where no current work plans and environmental assessments are in effect. As a result, ADC stopped control operations on eight districts, except in emergency situations. This action caused considerable reaction throughout the livestock industry, particularly the wool growers, because it occurred during the lambing season.

After:

> According to the Memorandum of Understanding between BLM and ADC, BLM is responsible for preparing environmental documents pursuant to the National Environmental Policy Act (NEPA). Adequate documents

have not been completed for all BLM districts, and some appeals were filed by environmental organizations. On April 6,1993, BLM instructed their State Directors to have APHIS cease ADC activities where no current work plans and environmental assessments are in effect. As a result, ADC stopped control operations on eight districts, except in emergency situations. This action caused considerable reaction throughout the livestock industry, particularly the wool growers, because it occurred during the lambing season.

Tactic 41: Create a Readable, Accessible Page

Sometimes writers are told what page formats to use and are even forced to enter their text into boxes on forms. With the exception of such cases, International English should use lots of white space. A 4½- or 5-inch column of text is far more likely to be read with understanding than a 6½- or 7-inch column.

By now, everyone can use readable, proportional typefaces with good x-heights (the height of the lower-case *x*). Although the Times New Roman font is not an especially readable typeface, it is a safe choice for electronically shared documents because nearly everyone has it installed. Since almost every document is likely to be stored or transmitted electronically, there is a recurring conflict between choosing the most readable fonts and choosing those that are found on most of the world's computers. *Word, Adobe Acrobat,* the various *ML* languages, as well as other publishing programs, give authors the option to embed their fonts within the document. This practice ensures the desired look of the publication but makes the file considerably larger. Where file size is not a problem, authors should take responsibility for the look of the received document. In other situations—slow Internet connections, for example—the larger files may be a significant inconvenience.

(Nowadays, most E1 business writers use the words *typeface* and *font* interchangeably; technically, this is an error. A font is an instance of a typeface; Arial is a typeface; Arial 12-point bold is a font.)

All companies, especially those that produce sophisticated publications with many graphics, should refrain from using elaborate, ornate, or high-concept typefaces. Though pleasing to the E1 eye, they are frustrating to the E2 reader and sometimes even impenetrable. Similarly, odd combinations of colors, like black text on dark red backgrounds, simply make everything harder to process, especially for those men with the most common form of color blindness. This tactic also applies to signs, package art, and store designs. International customers cannot be expected to choose your products and services if they cannot decipher the artistic lettering over your storefront or on your website.

A well-made International English page also uses frequent, helpful section names and subheadings. Wherever possible, the E2 reader is guided through the material with navigational aids. Long sections are shortened; cryptic chapter headings (*Introduction*) are enlarged to contain substance and information (*How to Register*). Consider these alternative Tables of Contents:

Before:
Introduction
Scheduling Alternatives
Decision Schedule
Attachments
After:
A Plan to Increase Tourism
What We Can Accomplish This Year
Approval Needed by July 1
Attachments: Scope of Work and Contract Forms

Generally, headings that contain one noun or a short string of nouns are clear only to their author and do not help the reader find needed passages or anticipate what is coming next. These headings are best replaced with fuller language: clauses, even whole sentences (for example, *We need a decision before July 1*) as a heading or subject line. Exceptions are documents localized for German readers of English, for whom a noun string is a familiar part of their syntax.

In International English documents, the more *side headings and marginal glosses* the better. Marginal glosses contain a terse summary of the adjacent paragraph, or sometimes a "pull quote" or "call out"—that is, a sentence or passage from the text that distills its meaning. Material in the margins serves many functions: it points the readers to the right paragraphs, it allows them to gloss over information they do not need to read, and it reinforces the central theme of the paragraph.

The use of side headings and marginal material also has the added benefit of forcing the main text into a narrower column. Consider the following example, a specimen culled from an old project file, chosen because it is made difficult to read by both its scientific content and its administrative/bureaucratic terminology. The exhibit is rendered even more unnecessarily burdensome by its format: a mono-spaced (nonproportional) typeface in a long, justified paragraph.

Before:

Currently our regulations 7 CFR 319.37 prohibit the importation of plants in growing media, with some exceptions. The prohibition on plants in soil and growing media goes back to the early days of plant quarantine in the U.S. as soil has historically been regarded as a dangerous agent for pest dispersal. We currently allow nine different kinds of plants to be imported in growing media under specific criteria found in 319.73–8 which must be met by the exporting country. None of the kinds of plants China wishes to export in media are currently approved. They originally asked that we consider in excess of 24 different types plants for shipment to the US. We asked that they prioritize their request and limit it to 5 or 6 of the more commonly exported types. Currently they export significant numbers of bare rooted penjing plants to the U.S. Shipping losses are realized from shock to root systems when media is removed and quarantine treatment at ports of entry due to the presence of quarantine pests. Prior to adding new kinds of plants to the already approved list APHIS must complete a pest risk assessment (pra) and follow the assessment with rulemaking provided that the assessment is favorable. Our experience with admitting new plants in media over the years has been unfavorable. Industry has challenged every attempt to add new genera of plants to our regulations. The Professional Plant Growers Association (PPGA) is seeking a court reversal of our last revision to Q-37 to add four additional genera to the list of approved plants to be imported in a growing medium.

The revision below does not alter a single sentence of the original; the changes are:

- Proportional typefaces
- Side headings
- Short paragraphs
- Boldface emphasis of key phrases
- Transitional words and phrases

After:
Plants in growing media are prohibited

Currently, our regulations (7 CFR 319.37) prohibit the importation of plants in growing media, historically regarded as a dangerous agent for pests. We currently allow nine exceptions, plants that may be imported in growing media under specific criteria that must be met by the exporting country (319.73-8).

China requests exceptions

None of the kinds of plants China wishes to export in media is currently approved. They originally asked that we consider more than 24 types of plants for shipment to the U.S. We asked that they select their 5 or 6 most commonly exported types. Currently they export significant numbers of bare rooted penjing plants to the U.S. Shipping losses result from shock to root systems when medium is removed, and also from quarantine treatment at ports of entry when we detect pests.

Plant industry resists all exceptions

Before adding new kinds of plants to the already approved list, APHIS must complete a pest risk assessment (pra) and, if the assessment is favorable, follow with rulemaking. Our experience with admitting new plants in media over the years has been unfavorable. Industry has challenged every attempt to add new genera of plants to our regulations.

For example, the Professional Plant Growers Association (PPGA) is seeking a court reversal of our last revision to Q-37, which added 4 genera to the list of plants approved to be imported in a growing medium.

Most readers will agree that, asked to edit or translate the passage above, they would clearly prefer the revised version. Again, all of the improvements involve format and presentation, not the diction or grammar.

Tactic 42: Reduce GOTOs

Reading is a linear process. No matter how words are organized on a page, in a book, or on a screen, the only way we can read a pair of words is *one after the other*. Therefore, the reading skill required to interpret a difficult passage or document is affected by how much work is needed to put the words in the proper sequence. The more branching, skipping, looping, and detouring—the more often the reader is compelled to read anything other than the next word on the page or screen—the less usable, the more stressful the document is.

I call all these discontinuities and nonlinearities with the programming term GOTOs—an instruction to branch off to another place in the program without indicating a clear path back to the departure point. Whenever possible, the number of GOTOs should be reduced in complicated texts, especially for an international audience. The E1 writer, among many other things, must therefore be aware of where pages break and must always place figures and exhibits as close to their first mention in the text as possible—preferably on the same page or on a facing page. Misplaced figures send readers to the next or previous page, or even to another section. They, along with glossary searches, tend to be the biggest branches.

GOTOs can come in any size, ranging from syntax errors that force a single sentence to be reread, to badly designed suites of publications that shunt readers to several volumes in a single seating. If feasible, then, International English documents should avoid

- Footnotes and endnotes: Place references directly in the text that mentions them. Footnotes are generally better than endnotes because the GOTO is smaller and easier to return from.
- Forward and backward references: Resist the use of "as mentioned earlier," "as explained above," and "discuss later." Although following this advice may lead to discussion of the same material twice or more times in the same document, and perhaps to inconsistencies and errors if the redundant passages are not updated simultaneously, it also reduces the E2's burden.

- Branching to other chapters and texts: If possible, readers should not have to leave the current place in the document to consult other sections or chapters. It should rarely be necessary to consult a second document while learning a single process or concept.
- "See Figure 1": When the reader is told to see Figure 1, Figure 1 should be visible, without turning pages: the graphic should be either on the same page or on the facing page. Although most business documents are printed on one side of the paper, placing charts, tables, figures, and other exhibits facing the text that discusses them greatly eases the reader's task.

Again, the key to reducing GOTOs seems to be repetition: repeating passages rather than sending the readers back and forth. The most important key, however, is to distinguish between narrative/instructional writing (where the reader wants to read words in sequence) and reference material (where the reader wants to find a small item, read it, and leave the text). GOTOs are a far more serious problem in narrative/instructional material, which often simply cannot work when the reader is forced to skip, branch, and loop around the text. Be aware, though, that *when experts write for nonexperts they usually create reference material (what the expert needs) and not instructional narratives (what the beginner, nonexpert needs).*

Hypertext and hypermedia eliminate most of the work associated with GOTOs. Readers can go anywhere in the document without turning pages and, more important, without getting lost. For any document that cannot be designed without extensive looping and branching, hypertext is preferable to print.

Tactic 43: Break Apart Long Paragraphs

Long sentences and paragraphs intimidate all readers, especially E2s. Even if a paragraph is logically cohesive, its length may discourage and frustrate the reader. The following paragraph (also justified to make it less inviting) is arbitrarily split. Notice the effect.

Before:
Remember that nearly all readers subvocalize, saying words mentally to themselves as they read silently. So, words that are hard to pronounce will slow the reader. This advice is particu-

larly germane in *naming* products, systems, or companies. Nearly every E2 and E3 has trouble with the *th* sound (especially unvoiced) and many Asian languages struggle with l and *r.* When General Instrument Corporation of Horsham, Pennsylvania, changed their image in 1996, they also adopted the more high-tech sounding name of NextLevel. In 1998, they will restore the original name, mainly because most of their Asian customers for cable-TV converter boxes have trouble with saying NextLevel. (Similarly, the spokesclown for McDonalds restaurants in Japan is called *Donald McDonald* not *Ronald.*)

After:

Remember that nearly all readers subvocalize, saying words mentally to themselves as they read silently. So, words that are hard to pronounce will slow the reader. This advice is particularly germane in *naming* products, systems, or companies. Nearly every E2 and E3 has trouble with the *th* sound (especially unvoiced) and many Asian languages struggle with l and *r.*

When General Instrument Corporation of Horsham, Pennsylvania, changed their image in 1996, they also adopted the more high-tech sounding name of NextLevel. In 1998, they will restore the original name, mainly because most of their Asian customers for cable-TV converter boxes have trouble with saying NextLevel. (Similarly, the spokesclown for McDonalds restaurants in Japan is called *Donald McDonald* not *Ronald.*)

Tactic 44: Convert Some Paragraphs into Lists

Proposals or reports that contain items or steps in a process are far more understandable in list form.

Instead of

In evaluating alternative offerors, please consider that our company has 15 years' experience in the construction of oil and gas pipelines. We hold the patents on the most advanced pumping technology. Further, we maintain business offices in all the major Middle Eastern capitals.

Write

In evaluating alternative offerors, please consider that our company

• Has 15 years' experience in the construction of oil and gas pipelines

- Holds the patents on the most advanced pumping technology
- Maintains business offices in all the major Middle Eastern capitals.

Tactic 45: Convert Some Paragraphs into Tables

For most readers, the most difficult paragraphs to understand are those that describe decision logic: options, alternatives, and multiple paths. Such passages tend to exhaust the attention of an E1 reader and create numerous opportunities for error and misinterpretation for an E2 reader. The following illustration converts a paragraph from a product manual into a clear table. In most cultures, a simple table will be far easier to follow.

Instead of:

New users should open the Maintenance Menu and select Setup. Also, old users may select Setup from the Maintenance Menu if they want to change their Preferences. Old users who don't want to change their setup in any way should go to the File menu and select either New or Open (for existing file).

Prefer:

User	Menu	Select . . .
New User	Maintenance	Setup
User wanting to change preferences	Maintenance	Setup
Other users	File	New (new file) OR Open (existing file)

Tactic 46: Convert Some Paragraphs into Playscripts

Playscript is a technique used to render a great range of instructions, specifications, and procedures into readable tables.

Before:

To get access to the files of another user on the LAN, you must get the owner of the files to grant written permission, specifying your read/write privileges on Form MIS89–10. This form must be sent to the LAN Administrator who, after receiving the form, has 5 days to create the software links necessary, consistent

with the read/write privileges. (For read-only links, the LAN
Administrator must respond within 3 days.) Upon receipt of
an e-mail bulletin from the Administrator, you may access the
designated files.

After:

Actor	Action
Applicant	1. Tells file owner of access request
	2. Completes form MIS89-10
	2a. If denied, advises applicant
LAN Administrator	3. Creates necessary software link
	3a. If read/write, within 5 days
	3b. If read-only, within 3 days
Applicant	4. Sends e-mail bulletin to applicant
	5. Accesses the file, as needed

Tactic 47: Convert Some Paragraphs into Decision Tables

To save space, technical communicators will often compress a branching procedure into a single paragraph. The following example shows
how much easier such a paragraph is to understand in the form of a tree
diagram.

Before:

You can create new subjects just as you create new collections by clicking Subject on the Options menu, then access-
ing File menu. You can also move subjects from one collection
to another by dragging them to the new collection, or you can
delete subjects from MM Manager by highlighting the subject
and clicking Delete on the Edit menu.

After:

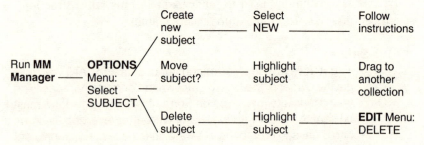

When text includes procedures, decision rules, and even branching paths, there are many other diagramming options as well. The following illustration shows the conversion of a paragraph into what is called a *logic box*, a graphical alternative to the decision tree, rendered more easily in a word processor.

Before:

> If you receive the "Illegal Access Attempt" message, determine whether you have mistyped the name of the file. (If you have, retype and continue.) If the file name has been typed correctly, review your access privileges by pressing <PF18> (or Alt+F8 if you are using a PC as a terminal). If you are denied access, you must contact the DB administrator to get your privileges changed. If you are not denied access, call the Help Desk for consultation.

After:

> Assure that the file name is typed correctly; then . . .

IF you are using	THEN press	AND IF you receive the message	THEN you should
A PC-terminal	ALT + F8	Denied	Call DB administrator
		Not denied	Call help desk
A standard terminal	PF18	Denied	Call DB administrator
		Not denied	Call help desk

Tactic 48: Convert Some Paragraphs into Logic Diagrams

An especially useful diagramming technique, the Nassi-Shneiderman chart, was developed in the 1970s as a flow-charting method for software engineers. It also works well to explain a wide variety of human and manual processes that involve decisions or iterations.

Before:

> Defining the Category of Failure
> The Manager of the Failure Analysis Laboratory determines the class of the failure, marks the sticker, and prepares a task document. In the case of bad subassemblies, he/she meets

with either the apposite DIGISOUND function or subcontractor. (No such meeting is required for defective contacts.) If the failure is from neither subassemblies, contacts, nor handling problems, the manager develops a High-Level Analysis Plan.

After:

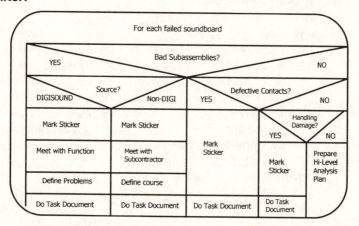

See Weiss, Edmond, "Visualizing a Procedure with Nassi-Shneiderman Charts," *Journal of Technical Writing and Communication*, Vol. 20(3): 1990.

Reducing Burdens as an Ethical Objective

Removing unnecessary burdens is an act of unselfishness, an extra exertion by the writer for the benefit of the reader. Granted, many of these extra exertions are meant to be a form of enlightened self-interest or deferred gratification. The rewards are downstream a bit. Even so, my experience is that the writers most likely to take time and pains with their work, to make the extra editorial sweep or two through the text, are those who genuinely care for their readers and who want them to have the easiest reading experience possible.

Caring about the reader is a difficult emotion to counterfeit, as is seeming to be sincerely interested in another country when your motive is obviously short-term profit. Good communicating, as Quintilian once observed, needs good people.

Discussion Questions

• Do you find yourself skimming nearly everything you read? Does this prevent you from getting what you need from the documents? What might prevent you from skimming?

- In your school or business reading, have you ever noticed differences in the style of the writers you must read: specifically, that some seemed unnecessarily harder to read than others, even though they were writing about similar matters?
- In your school or business reading, have you ever noticed differences in the layout and organization of textbooks and other documents: specifically, that some seemed unnecessarily harder to use than others?
- When you have difficulty following written instructions, do you tend to blame yourself or the writer?
- When you prepare longer documents—reports, proposals, manuals, and so on—do you worry about where the pages break? where the figures and tables appear in relation to the text that discussed them?
- Acquire and read a copy of the Security & Exchange Commission's *Plain English Handbook* (www.sec.gov/pdf/handbook.pdf). Do you believe all financial and business documents should follow this guide? Is anything in this guide unsuitable for International English?

Sources and Resources

Andrews, Deborah C. (ed.). *International Dimensions of Technical Communication.* Arlington, VA: Society for Technical Communication, 1996.

Andrews, D. C. *Technical Communication in the Global Community.* Upper Saddle River, NJ: Prentice-Hall, 1998.

Barzun, Jacques. *Simple and Direct: A Rhetoric for Writers.* Revised ed. Chicago: University of Chicago Press, 1985.

Brockmann, R. John. *Writing Better Computer User Documentation: From Paper to Hypertext.* Version 2.0. New York: John Wiley & Sons, 1990.

Casady, Mona, and Lynn Wasson. "Written Communication Skills of International Business Persons." *The Bulletin of ABC 57,* no. 4 (1994) 36–40.

Garbl's Grammar Webpage (http://garbl.home.comcast.net/writing/grammar.htm)

Hoft, Nancy L. *International Technical Communication: How to Export Information about High Technology.* New York: John Wiley & Sons, 1995.

(Nancy Hoft's website, http://www.world-ready.com, may be the best single resource for students of international communication.)

Horn, Robert E. *Visual Language: Global Communication for the 21st Century.* Bainbridge Island, WA: MacroVU Press, 1998.

Huckin, Thomas N., and Leslie A. Olsen. *Technical and Professional Communication for Nonnative Speakers of English.* 2nd ed. Boston: McGraw-Hill, 1991.

Jones, Scott, Cynthia Kennelly, Claudia Mueller, Marcia Sweezey, Bill Thomas, and Lydia Velez. *Digital Guide to Developing International User Information.* Maynard, MA: Digital Press, 1992.

Kohl, John R. "Using 'Syntactic Clues' to Enhance Readability for Nonnative Speakers of English." *Society for Technical Communication, Proceedings of the 38th Annual Conference* (1991) 54–571.

Menand, Louis. "Bad Comma." *The New Yorker,* June 28, 2004, p. 103.

Nielsen, Jakob, and Marie Tahir. *Homepage Usability: 50 Websites Deconstructed.* Indianapolis, IN: New Riders Publishing, 2001.

Schriver, Karen A. *Dynamics in Document Design.* New York: John Wiley & Sons, 1997.

Victor, David A. "Advancing Research in International Business Communication." *The Bulletin of ABC,* 57, no. 3 (1994) 41–42.

Ward, James. "Editing in a Bilingual, Bicultural Context." *Journal of Technical Writing and Communication* 18, no. 39 (1988) 221–226.

Weiss, Edmond. *How to Write Usable User Documentation.* 2nd ed. Scottsdale, AZ: Greenwood/Oryx Press, 1991.

5

Writing for Translation

*In a sense, all International English is written for
translation. Unlike that rare reader who can think and
speak fluently in more than one language, the E2 reader
should be presumed to be translating, slowly, in real time.
Thus, every principle and tactic that makes International
English more accessible to E2s will make it more easily
translated as well. The objective of this chapter, therefore,
is to illustrate that the more structured and controlled one's
English, the more straightforward the translation;
furthermore, that fully controlled English makes machine
translation an imperfect but practical option.*

Limits on Translation

Some people believe that translation is an impossibility. They are correct, if what is meant by translation is a perfect rendering of the text
with nuance and tone identical to the original. In literature, translation
can be most unsatisfying; many agree that reading poetry in translation
is, in R.S. Thomas's apt phrase, "like kissing through a handkerchief."
Interestingly, Israeli writer Bialak said that translation was like "kissing
a bride through a veil." (Of course, he said it in Hebrew.) And speaking
of Hebrew . . . Rabbi Mordechai Kaplan once observed that the difference between reading the Pentateuch (the first five books of the Bible)

in Hebrew and in translation was like the difference between visiting Italy and seeing a travelogue film about Italy.

Obviously, when language has a poetic dimension, when the sound and rhythm contribute to the meaning, when there are echoes and connotations swirling around the words, translation fails to capture the original. Even the best translations of the Hebrew Scriptures, for example, make almost no effort to recreate the puns and wordplay in the Hebrew, pursuing a prosaic literalness instead. That is why English poets who have put their talents to translation, from Alexander Pope to Robert Pinsky, have attempted to create a poetic alternative—a good English poem with semantic links to the original Latin or Italian or other language being translated.

But it is not just poetry that eludes translation. Even ordinary prose in any natural language is so laced with idiom and allusion, so dependent on a deeply ingrained knowledge of sentence structures and rhythms, that even the translation of a software update procedure or a government regulation can lose more than a little in translation. My Canadian colleagues claim that they can always tell which of the two versions, French or English, was the original and which the translation. When they find the translation makes no sense, they will switch to reading the original language, even if that is not the language they prefer. That is, E1s who are F2s (Anglophones who read French as their second language) claim to find idiomatic French easier to understand than badly written English.

Not surprisingly, many students of language are skeptical about the possibilities of translation. Anthropologists who study language (e.g., Hall and Hall, 1990) insist that language and culture are so deeply intertwined that different languages represent different ways of apprehending the world.

In this connection, undergraduates are especially charmed by what is called the Whorf-Sapir Linguistic Relativity Hypothesis (Whorf, 1956)—the notion that people can only perceive the phenomena they have words for. In the most famous example, the Eskimos (today the Inuit) have so many words for snow that we may infer, first, that snow is an essential part of their lives and, second, that they can perceive many more kinds of snow than the English speaker, who is limited to *snow* and *slush*. (English, in contrast, has a large nuanced vocabulary of words that pertain to beating: *beat, spank, flog, whip, whisk, task, lash, thrash, flay, belabor, chastise, cane*, etc. I wonder what anthropological inference should be drawn.) The truth is, however, as Geoffrey Pullum (1991) explains, the Eskimos have relatively few words for snow—only three or four, in fact—and even if they had a dozen or twenty, it would be entirely unremarkable and mundane.

People who live in and work with snow would, of course, have a bigger snow vocabulary than people who do not, just as a window maker would know what a "triple-sash double-hung" window is and be able to name its several dozen parts. Indeed, my skier friends have no trouble differentiating eight or ten different kinds of snow in English, each with a special implication for their skiing plans.

Speculation about these impenetrable cultural barriers is interesting and sensitizes those who underestimate the complexities of even routine translation. But too much of this rumination can distract us from the fact that *good enough translation happens all the time.*

Translation Is a Business Expense

Nearly all International English is translated by the E2 reader. Although some tactics (like the hyphenation of unit modifiers) are helpful to human readers but confusing to some software-assisted translation, generally everything that simplifies, clarifies, and reduces burdens for the E2 reader will also facilitate translation. Note also that the professional translator (writing) or interpreter (speech) is usually translating from English into his or her native language. United Nations interpreters, I am told, may translate *only* into their own native language, and, since the UN is the gold standard for translation, we may assume that the best translators of English are E2 readers as well.

Not surprisingly, everyone who writes on this subject begins with an injunction to write simply and clearly. In addition, among the tactics most often cited by professional translators and translation services as being helpful to translation are:

- Repetition of nouns (rather than relying on backward-pointing pronouns)
- Close proximity of modifiers to the things they modify
- Use of optional relative pronouns (especially *that* and *which*)
- Use of all articles, even in lists, tables, and diagrams
- Use of words with their first or most common definition
- Avoidance of homographic words like *secretive* (pertaining either to secrets or secretions)

Making these extra editorial sweeps through a document takes time, just as do all the other tactics recommended in this text. They therefore represent an added expense, even before the considerable expense of translation itself. Given that some companies do not even bother to translate their business documents and product literature at all, why should others not only translate but make expensive preparations for translation?

The answer is they should not—unless such actions are perceived as legitimate business expenses, either necessary or worthwhile. In some circumstances national laws compel companies to translate their labels, packages, and product literature into a specified language. In Canada, for example, every box of breakfast cereal and headache remedy must have English and French labeling, even when the product is being sold in those Canadian provinces with more German or Ukrainian speakers than French. Although this may constitute an irritating cost for those companies whose sales or customer relations will not thereby benefit, it is still a smart investment to serve the needs of several million customers who might otherwise avoid the product.

Interestingly, the proportion of Americans who speak Spanish, primarily or exclusively, is comparable to the proportion of Canadians who speak French. Yet, only a handful of American companies or products include Spanish labels or product directions, and those are said to be "targeting" the Latino market.

Translation, like all issues related to corporate communication and documentation, is a business issue. As a communication consultant, the first question I ask my clients is: How is business, and what, if anything, can your company's communications do to improve business? The point of this question is that, while, on the one hand, translation seems to be a matter of editing syntax and localizing date and money conventions, on the other hand it involves using business resources cost effectively or profitably. *And often the advocates for International English and translation fail to make a business case to accompany their technical recommendations.*

Again, companies translate either because they have to or because they choose to. Those people in the company who want quality translation must first research the most attractively priced, qualified translation service or contractor. They must also build a business case showing that the benefits of the translation, or other language improvements, exceed the cost. Business cases are like internal proposals: justifications for proposed expenses. Unfortunately, the language enthusiasts in an organization are often perceived as having technical and aesthetic interests without sufficient appreciation for the "bottom line." And if they offer no business argument for their expensive requests or recommendations they deserve that reputation.

The two main justifications for a business expenditure are:

- To get more or better customers and clients
- To lower the cost of doing business

Translation can sometimes yield both of these results by, for example, making a product more attractive in a market than the competitor's untranslated product or by reducing the cost of customer services caused by customers struggling with instructions or manuals.

When translation is perceived as a requirement or constraint, unrelated to sales or efficiency, we should not be surprised when the corporate goal is to do it as cheaply as possible, satisfying the requirement without concern for quality.

Preparing a Manuscript for Translation

When preparing a manuscript, it may be necessary to adjust, exaggerate, or even undo some of the tactics used to make it readable to E2s. For example, translators are put off by parentheses, especially those within a sentence. The advice to never break words at the ends of lines applies particularly to translation, especially when there is some machine- or software-assisted translation involved. Before sending a manuscript to a translator, one should disable automatic hyphenation and, in fact, disable automatic everything, including the spacing after punctuation marks. Translators prefer the traditional one space after a comma and two spaces after a period or other end punctuation. Microsoft Word plays with these spacing conventions, unless instructed not to. Similarly, automatic translators, like many optical character readers, are tripped up by dashes and underscored words. Some translation agencies will strip the em- and en-dashes from the manuscript, along with many hyphenated terms.

Perhaps the best thing the author of a document can do for a translator is to leave sufficient white space, not just in the body of the text but in the headlines, side headings, and caption spaces of the figures. Because spelling conventions vary widely among languages, not uncommonly the translated version will need appreciably more space than the English version. For example, French averages about 30 percent more characters than English and also needs a bit more space between lines (leading) to allow for accents in the ascender and descender areas of the typeface. As was mentioned in the discussion of burdens, almost every reader on earth prefers white space to dense prose text.

The authors of the original document should also indicate whether certain portions of the text are to be left untranslated. When product and company names contain ordinary English words like Home Depot or House of Pancakes, the translation software—even a human translator—may replace the words with those from the other language. Also, if there is a "tag line" or other bit of marketing copy attached to the product or company name, the authors may want to mark that DO NOT TRANSLATE as well. Unless warned otherwise, translation software or naïve translators will translate the individual, uncapitalized words in a technical term (like *multiple virtual storage* or *balance sheet*), with bizarre results. For example, they have been known to translate persons' names, in those cases where the name was also an English word (e.g., Smith).

It is not enough that certain words, such as proper nouns, are capitalized, therefore untranslated. Not all the untranslated terms will be capitalized; sometimes every word in a document or passage is capitalized, leaving the translator still unsure about what to leave untranslated. The responsibility is with the originator of the document to develop a convention (color, font, tag) that keeps certain words in English. (Although research shows that it takes longer for E1s to read a document that is all upper case letters, some consideration might be given to the tradition of teaching upper case letters first to those learning a new alphabet. This might make capitalized messages easier to read for E2s whose first language does not use the Roman alphabet.)

Conventions that *must* be evaluated in every translated document are as follows:

- Date formats. What does 5/6/05 mean?
- Units of measurement. Metric, English? How much is a ton, or tonne?
- Numbering Schemes. How many millions in a billion?
- Numeric Conventions. How are commas and decimal points used as separators in large numbers?

- Currency Conventions. How are commas and decimal points used as separators in currency? What symbols are used to represent the various currencies? How are U.S. dollars differentiated from other dollars?
- Local Abbreviations and Acronyms. Expressions such as IRA and ATM mean different things in different settings.
- Reserved or Restricted Characters. Have such symbols as @, #, \, or ~ been assigned special meanings or software interpretations? Are certain characters reserved and restricted, or even missing from popular foreign character sets?
- Alphabetization. How will translation affect the usability of alphabetized lists that are no longer in alphabetical order?

Localized translations must also be cognizant of another metrics issue: the widespread preference throughout the world for the A4 paper size (and the four-ring loose-leaf binder), which may distort the intended design, layout, and page breaks of the original.

These localization issues are mostly mechanical; many of them can be programmed into the translation software. But there are other recurring localization issues, most notably the *voice* of the document. For example, John Brockmann (1990) points out that the preferred form for technical instructions in America, the imperative, may be inappropriate in certain cultures. So, *Enter your clearance code* becomes *The operator enters his or her clearance code.*

Incidentally, "his or her" is less an issue around the world than in English-speaking countries. Most modern natural languages assign one of two or three genders to every noun and sometimes to every attached adjective and article. For example, in most languages, there is a male and female form for *worker,* but *workers* is usually masculine. English speakers, who have only six gender-marked words (*he, him, his, she, her, hers*), are far more sensitive about gender stereotyping than those whose languages have thousands of gender-marked words.

Controlled Language and the Future of Translation

One of my favorite bits of science fiction technology is Douglas Adams's Babel Fish (*The Hitchhiker's Guide to the Galaxy*), a small creature inserted into the human ear, after which all incoming messages received by the owner of that ear will be translated in real time into the owner's language.

Automatic translation, like teleportation, is a fantasy concept, necessary in works of fiction and film, in which people must not only be able to move faster than the speed of light but also must be able to converse with people from anywhere else—including other species from other parts of the galaxy. The reality of natural languages, however, is that real-time perfect translation will always be a novelist's fantasy. For example, here is a German-to-English translation by a program called, interestingly enough, Babel Fish:

German Original
US-Verbraucherpreise steigen stärker als erwartet
(Source: Süddeutsche Zeitung, February 21, 2001)

Washington, 21. Feb (Reuters)-Hohe Energiekosten haben die Verbraucherpreise in den USA im Januar überraschend deutlich ansteigen lassen und so Analysten zufolge die Wahrscheinlichkeit schneller kräftiger Leitzinssenkungen durch die US-Notenbank Fed gedämpft. Die Teuerung stieg im Januar zum Vormonat um 0,6 Prozent nach 0,2 Prozent im Dezember 2000, teilte das Arbeitsministerium am Mittwoch in Washington mit. Von Reuters befragte Volkswirte hatten im Durchschnitt nur mit einem Anstieg von 0,3 Prozent gerechnet. Das US-Handelsministerium teilte zudem mit, das Außenhandelsdefizit in den USA habe im Gesamtjahr 2000 mit 369,7 Milliarden Dollar (791 Milliarden DM) einen Rekordwert erreicht. Der Euro stieg nach der Veröffentlichung der US-Daten auf ein vorläufiges Tageshoch von 0,9181 Dollar, bröckelte im weiteren Verlauf jedoch wieder etwas ab.

Babel Fish Machine Translation:
US consumer prices rise more strongly than expected

Washington, 21 February (Reuters)-high energy costs surprisingly clearly in such a way absorbed the consumer prices in the USA in January rise to let and according to Analysten the probability of fast strong key interest lowerings by the US issuing bank Fed. The price increase rose in January to the previous month by 0,6 per cent after 0,2 per cent in December 2000, indicated the Ministry of Labour on Wednesday in Washington. Political economists asked by Reuters had counted on the average only on a rise of 0,3 per cent. The US Ministry of Trade indicated besides, the foreign trade deficit in the USA has in the whole year 2000 with 369.7 billion dollar (791 billion DM) a record value achieved. The euro rose after the publication of the US data to a provisional daily high of 0.9181 dollar, crumbled in the further process however again somewhat off.

Machine translation results do not have to be quite so bad as this one. But even sophisticated and expensive services can produce unsatisfying results. *Newsday* reported the problems Suffolk County, New York, government officials experienced when they used machine translation to produce Spanish versions of their election ballot. Among other problems, the software translated Board (as in Board of Elections) as *tablero,* which is a board made of wood, rather than *consejo, junta,* or *commission.*

Despite such results, more than a few futurists still believe that good enough automatic translation will be available within the next generation or two. Ray Kurzweil (1998), a persuasive futurist and genius inventor, predicts that we will have translating telephones, capable of instantaneous voice translation for several language pairs, by 2009. Machine translation of speech is even more problematical, of course, a fact that everyone who has worked with Kurzweil's speech recognition software can attest to.

When computer-based translation research began in the 1960s, it was based on a set of false assumptions and limited by prevailing technology. It falsely assumed that the grammar of a sentence was in the surface of the sentence, the particular words in a particular order. But Noam Chomsky and others explained that the grammar of the sentence is not in the string of words but in the set of operations, or transformations, that put the sentence together. In a famous example, *John is eager to please.* and *John is easy to please.* are two sentences with nearly identical surfaces but different meanings. In the first, John pleases others, whereas in the second others please John. How could a mere computer program, limited to scanning the words, "know" what the sentences meant? And, so, how could it translate them into other languages?

When early machine translation programs converted a passage from Language 1 into Language 2, and then back from Language 2 into Language 1, the results were typically laughable, and, according to most language theorists, inevitable.

But that was then. It was a time when it was said that a computer with enough memory to play chess would be as big as the Empire State Building. It was also a time when the emphasis in software development was on *heuristics*, intelligent routines that would enable the program to find the best of several million combinations by searching only a few thousand possibilities. The rationale for heuristics, of course, was that problems with several billion alternative solutions would never be solved, even by the most powerful computer. (Like heuristic programming, some of today's translation software performs a process called *gisting*, extracting the gist of a message without precise translation.)

Raw computing power and cheap computing resources simplify life for the programmer. There is no need to conserve resources or find an alternative to running a billion alternatives. Today's least expensive computers can spell-check from a 50,000-word dictionary in an instant and plot an optimum cross-country driving plan almost as fast. Will there ever come a day when a translation program will be able to do more than parse the surface of a sentence and make substitutions of one lexicon for another? When it will search an immense library of words and phrases to look for similarities with the current context and bring that context to the translation? When it will recognize a literary or biblical allusion and find a high-quality translation of the original in its own language and insert it? When it will draw inferences about the age, education, sophistication, and general style of the writer and concoct a translated persona with similar traits, manifest in the translated version?

If reading a poem in translation is like kissing a bride through a veil, then reading a poem in machine translation is like kissing through chain mail. Still, it is evident that, as the years pass, more and more professional and commercial translation will be done by software, while other software is busy extracting passages and modules that have already been translated from well-ordered text databases. Professional translators, masters of one of the most intellectually demanding of all professions, will increasingly be people who supervise the mechanical translation and, at the end, "tweak" the errors made by the tin-eared software.

Corporations, especially American ones, have never been happy about paying for translation services and are, therefore, rushing the technology. They are willing to accept the cheapest machine translation, even if it is not yet good enough to represent their business interests. It follows, then, that the more a company's English is controlled, the more it resembles Caterpillar English or AECMA's Simplified English, the more likely it is to be understood by E2s and translated accurately by translation software. A very brief Internet search suggests that there are several Simplified Chinese systems also available, presumably mapped onto their Simplified English counterparts.

As indicated in the chapter on simplification, organizations can either adopt a complete, official, software-enabled controlled language or, at the least, adopt a restricted vocabulary and a set of simplifying standards of grammar and usage, enforced by style software or editors. Here, for example, are some of the rules of Simplified English:

- Use approved words only as the part of speech given. (For example: *close* is a verb [and not an adverb].)
- Write: Do not go near the landing gear if . . . (NOT: Do not go close to the landing gear if . . .)
- You can use the verb in these tenses: the infinitive, the present tense, the past tense, the simple future tense, and the past participle (as an adjective). (For example: *To adjust; It adjusts; It adjusted; It will adjust. It is adjusted.*)
- The maximum length of a paragraph is 6 sentences.
- Do not use one-sentence paragraphs more than once in every ten paragraphs.

These rules, though arbitrary, are not unreasonable. It may well offend the sensibility of expert writers to submit to these standards, but it will not prevent them from writing good business and technical documents. And the translation will go much more smoothly.

Discussion Questions

- Have you read any documents that you suspect were translated by machine? What gave you that impression?
- Have your travel or business plans ever been upset by problems with dates, numbers, measures, or currency designations?
- As a writer, how do you feel about being required to limit yourself to certain words and grammatical forms? Would you worry less if your computer did the editing?
- Have you ever translated a document—outside a class in foreign language? Was the source language your first or second language? What was the experience like? Did your translation work?
- Have you ever worked on a project that was injured by a translation error?

Sources and Resources

Arnold, Doug. *Machine Translation: An Introductory Guide,* online at http://
www.essex.ac.uk/linguistics/clmt/Mtbook

Brockmann, John. *Writing Better Computer User Documentation.* 2nd ed. New York:
John Wiley & Sons, 1990.

Hall, Edward T., and Mildred Reed Hall. *Understanding Cultural Differences: Ger-
mans, French, and Americans.* Yarmouth, ME: Intercultural Press, 1990.

Kirkman, John, C. Snow, and I. Watson. "Controlled English as an Alternative to
Multiple Translation." *IEEE Transactions on Professional Communication,* PC-
21, no. 4 (1978) 159–161.

Kulik, Ann B. "How the Tech Writer Improves Translation Results." *Global Talk*—
Newsletter of the International Technical Communication Special Interest Group,
STC 3:1 (1995).

Kurzweil, Ray. *The Age of the Spiritual Machines.* New York: Penguin Books, 1998.

Lingo Systems. *The Guide to Translation and Localization.* Los Alamitos, CA: IEEE
Computer Society, 1999.

Maylath, Bruce."Writing Globally: Teaching the Technical Writing Student to Prepare Documents for Translation." *Journal of Business and Technical Communication* (July 1997) 339–352.

Pullum, Geoffrey. *The Great Eskimo Vocabulary Hoax.* Chicago: University of Chicago Press, 1991.

Robinson, Douglas. *Becoming a Translator: An Accelerated Course.* New York:
Routledge, 1997.

Rosseel, Peter, and Mary K. Roll. "Cross-Cultural Technical Translations: From an
Isolated Translator to a Business Communicator."*1990 Proceedings of the International Technical Communication Conference.* Arlington, VA: Society for Technical Communication, 1990, pp. RT-99 to RT-102.

Schulte, Rainer, and John Biguenet (eds.). *Theories of Translation: An Anthology of
Essays from Dryden to Derrida.* Chicago: University of Chicago Press, 1992.

Seguinot, Candace. "Technical Writing and Translation: Changing with the Times."
Journal of Technical Writing and Communication 24 (1994) 285–292.

Spyridakis, Jan, Heather Holmback, and Serena Shubert. "Measuring the Translat-
ability of Simplified English in Procedural Documents." *IEEE Transactions on
Professional Communication* 40 (1997) 4–12.

Translation Journal (online): http://accurapid.com/journal/

Vitek, Steve. "Reflections of a Human Translator on Machine Translation Or Will
MT Become the 'Deus Ex Machina' Rendering Humans Obsolete in an Age
When 'Deus Est Machina?'" *Translation Journal* 4 (July 2000). http://
accurapid.com/journal/

Weiss, Timothy. "Reading Culture: Professional Communication as Translation."
Journal of Business and Technical Communication (July 1997) 321–338.

Weiss, Timothy. "Translation in a Borderless World." *Technical Communication
Quarterly* 4, no. 4 (1995) 407–425.

Whorf, Benjamin Lee. *Language, Thought, and Reality.* New York: John Wiley &
Sons, 1956.

6

Principles of Correspondence

The ability to write a professional-sounding letter is a mark of business maturity. Business correspondence has a tone, pace, and attitude that takes some time to master; moreover, the largely unwritten rules of style differ markedly from country to country. The objective of this chapter, therefore, is to provide a framework for researching international correspondence cultures, as well as to caution against errors of style and etiquette that often afflict the letters and e-mails of North American business writers.

Business Letters: An Exercise in Style

Those of us who edit business communication would be just as happy if we never again saw the phrase *as per.* (*Per* is Latin for *as.*) Actually, we would not mind if *per* disappeared entirely from English business documents, except in such phrases as *miles-per-gallon.* This bit of adopted Latin (like *in re*) is an example of what I call *letter lingo*, words and phrases used by people writing memos or letters—and at no other time. Interestingly, no matter how often I urge my clients and students to replace these peculiar phrases (like *enclosed please find*), they resist. Their fear is that letters and memos without this stock parlance will not sound like real business writing, that omitting these words and phrases will make the writers appear inexperienced or unprofessional.

Although these fears are exaggerated, they do reflect the reality that part of being socialized into any professional culture, regardless of the country, is learning a new vocabulary (cant, argot, jargon, lingo, or patois) that defines one as an insider. In connection with letter and memo writing, there is not only a vocabulary but a structure—a standard sequence of parts/topics—as well as a small set of acceptable page layouts and formats. Not only do most image-conscious corporations take pains to design their letterhead (fancy name for *stationery*), they also usually specify the look, feel, and page layout as well: margins, tabs, typefaces/fonts, indentation, spacing, and location of letter elements on a page grid.

Now that possibly most business professionals type their own letters, it is harder than ever for companies to enforce their correspondence standards. Also, now that, at least in certain countries, e-mail exchanges —originally intended as little more than a replacement for short phone messages left on an answering machine—have begun to overwhelm all other forms of business correspondence, one might expect the imminent demise of the business letter as a sophisticated demonstration of good manners and professional language. Perhaps. But, as of this writing at least, in most of the world the business letter remains an exercise in style, a test of one's experience and one's ear for nuance.

Preparing international letters obliges E1 writers to think strategically about the mix of culture-free and culture-fair tactics in their messages. The differences across cultures—even within the larger countries—are not only many but also subtle. Toby Atkinson's indispensable Merriam-Webster's *International Business Communications* ably explains the scores of technical details that differentiate one country from another but says almost nothing about matters such as the appropriate tone to assume when breaking bad news to a partner, or whether that tone should be different for a French or Japanese audience. The style differences between countries are so subtle and elusive that, unless the E1 writer has the services of an expert consultant from the receiver's culture, it might be better to retain the sender's format and style, applying all the simplification, clarification, and culture-removing tactics mentioned so far.

The question that arises is whether to pursue the high-risk (therefore, potentially high-return) strategy of trying to write letters in the style of the recipient, even though it means considerable work, and even though there is a significant chance of error. Complicating matters is that the interpretation of your "failure" will also vary from country to country. In some countries, your effort will be appreciated, whereas in others your failure will seem insincere, even meretricious.

The other option, again, is to play it safe: write readable, International English in one's own format, knowing that the only penalty or "downside" is that one might give an advantage to the rival or competitor who uses the more difficult, localization strategy successfully.

Tactic 49: Eliminate Western Letter Lingo and Formats

Again, letter lingo refers to the special set of words (*per*), phrases (*enclosed find*), and syntax (*Should your travel plans* instead of *If your travel plans*) that seem to be used in correspondence and nowhere else. Apparently, the exclusive use of this small vocabulary in the formal letters of nearly every English-speaking country suggests that it is a legitimate part of the socialization of professional people in many professions. Oddly enough, nearly every teacher of business and professional writing urges against this style. Expressions such as *in re* or simply *re* (to mean *about* or *regarding*) are stilted, hackneyed, pretentious, and distracting. Els simply do not talk that way (although I have heard more than a few *per*s slip into conversations). Moreover, they usually do not write that way either—except in letters and memos.

The inclination to use this style is an understandable part of the desire to fit in, to sound like one of the group. Entry-level employees quickly notice their company's affectations of correspondence style and try to imitate them. So, for example, what would ordinarily be *last Thursday* is transmogrified into *Thursday last.* The mere fact that this style is noticeable and calls attention to itself should make it suspect to a thoughtful writer. Outside of the literary arts, good style should be invisible, never drawing attention from substance and meaning.

But what is the origin of the style itself? Why have so many gravitated toward this set of flat, boring verbal mannerisms? Probably, letter lingo emanates from the desire to sound as important and official as possible, especially in the opening line of the document. It is an imitation of how nonlawyers imagine lawyers write. But the style of writing generally disparaged as "legalese" is as disliked by good lawyers as by anyone else. Typically, when people try to impress their readers by imitating a lawyer, they end up imitating a mediocre or evasive lawyer instead. Usually, attempts to write in this style make one's letters sound

less like legal documents than like the stultifying reports of police officers and insurance adjusters, or the opening and closing speeches of flight
attendants—the only class of North American English speakers who
still make extensive use of the subjunctive mood, as in *should there be a
sudden change of cabin pressure.*

For those whose strategy is to write as simply and directly as possible, then, the first step is to replace letter lingo with plain English
alternatives:

> **Before:**
> Per your request of 25 May, I am providing herein a response
> to your complaints re missing items.
>
> **After:**
> Here is an explanation of the missing items described in your
> May 25 letter.

> **Before:**
> Enclosed please find our response pursuant to your inquiry of
> March last. We hereby advise you, as per your request, that
> we will be sending said refund in due course under separate
> cover.
>
> **After:**
> We have received and read your letter written last March. We
> agree that you are entitled to a refund, which we will send you
> in just a few days.

When possible, E1s should strike the words *enclosed, attached,* and
referenced from their correspondence. These stale, overused expressions—for example, *as referenced above*—are so predictable and uninteresting that they kill the attentiveness of the reader. They are most
evident, incidentally, in cover letters and letters of transmittal, documents in which the date is the only real information. So, *attached please
find* becomes *here is* or *this is.* If the goal is to produce a lean, culture-
free document, it is also best to refrain from stock expressions of cour-
tesy and politeness (*we regret, should the need arise, we trust*). In general,
expressing emotions with standardized expressions sounds insincere.

If the E1 sender has decided not to emulate the letter style of the
recipient, it may also be wise to eliminate the letter format altogether,
replacing it with a trim, unmannered document that more resembles a
memo. As already suggested in the earlier discussion on reducing burdens,

much of the material buried in paragraphs is better communicated to E2, and almost everyone else, as lists, tables, charts, or simple diagrams. But the letter format itself militates against these improvements. Although many letters contain lists, how many letters contain charts? or drawings?

The traditional letter is a prose-paragraph medium, loosely structured, a challenge for the reader. The modern memo, however, is a more tightly structured form, more comfortable with bullet lists and diagrams. Consider the following example, in which a typical, letter-lingo-filled, paragraph-based letter is replaced with a fully structured document:

Before:

Dear Task Force Members,

Pursuant to the questions raised at the last meeting of the Telecommunications Planning Team I have reviewed several alternative sites for our future meetings. This referenced the fact that several members of the Team found our Piscataway office inaccessible and inconvenient.

Per Todd's suggestion, I considered several options. Among these were a small office suite maintained by our company in Manhattan, our office in Pittsburgh, our office in Cincinnati, or hotel sites at the major New York airports: JFK, LaGuardia, and Newark. (I also weighed these sites against the current practice of holding the meetings here at HQ.) I evaluated these locations on several criteria. I was mainly interested in the travel time and travel costs for the Team members, but I was also concerned with the availability of the facilities and with whether they would have all the equipment and resources we use at our meetings, such as copy machines, fax hookups, etc.

What my analysis shows is that the cost of renting hotel space at an airport is much less than the added costs of car rentals, etc. Even if members from the Piscataway group have to drive to the meeting in a van, the savings in time and travel expenses are tremendous.

As a result I am recommending that we move the meetings to a hotel near JFK airport (either Embassy Suites or Courtyard). Since most of the team members fly USAir through JFK, this is the most convenient arrangement. We at Piscataway can bring some of the equipment we need in the van.

Should you have any reactions, please contact me at 201 . . . .

After:

TO: Members of the Telecommunications
                                 Planning Team

ABOUT: Need to Change Site of Team
                                 Meetings to JFK Airport

RECOMMENDATION: We should hold future team meetings
                     at an airport hotel near JFK Airport
                     (Embassy Suites or Courtyard)

BACKGROUND: The Piscataway meeting site is
                     inaccessible to everyone but people
                     who work at Piscataway.

ALTERNATIVES: • Manhattan office
                     • Pittsburgh office
                     • Cincinnati office
                     • Newark Airport
                     • LaGuardia Airport
                     • JFK Airport
                     • Piscataway office (status quo)

CRITERIA: • Travel time for participants
                     • Travel costs for participants
                     • Availability of facilities
                     • Cost of facilities
                     • Resources available at site (copier,
                       fax, etc.)

ANALYSIS: I recommend the JFK site for the
                     following reasons:
                     • It is best for all but the Piscataway
                       members (3 of 9).
                     • It costs much less than the travel
                       costs it saves.
                     • It is the most available plan.
                     • The lack of resources can be
                       accommodated by bringing equip-
                       ment from Piscataway.

ACTION: Please write, fax, or e-mail at once to
                     say whether you approve or disap-
                     prove of this plan.

Almost any reader would prefer the latter version, especially since the gist of it can be learned from reading no more than the subject line. But there are many situations—perhaps most—when such an austere, undecorated message would communicate the wrong attitude and deference.

Tactic 50: Adopt the Receiver's Format

To localize the format of a letter for a particular E2 country, E1 can either consult one of the published compendiums of international styles, such as the Merriam-Webster guide mentioned earlier, study a text devoted to the business practices of the particular country, or merely collect a few samples, most usefully from the company you intend to write to. With this material in hand, the next step is to develop a sample or model to follow, a template, with illustrations of the following items:

- General Page Appearance—How much of the page, and which parts, should be allocated to headings and documentation, as opposed to body text; how much white space; what typefaces, leading (spacing), and font size?
- Letterhead Conventions—Where should the identification of the sender's organization appear; what is an appropriate size; what colors are inappropriate; how commercial should the headers and footers be (would it be too brash to include tag lines in the letterhead, for example); what information should be provided?
- Date Line—Where should the date appear; in what format?
- Internal Address—Where should the recipient's name and address appear; what titles, honorifics, or position descriptions should be included; should any information other than the mailing address be included, like e-mail and fax information? (Note: Under no circumstances should any business letter misspell the name of its recipient; any cost required to verify title, name, and spelling is well spent.)
- Return Address—Where, other than the letterhead, should the sender's return address appear; should any information other than the mailing address be included (like e-mail and fax information)?
- Subject Line(s)—Should the letter contain one or more subject lines; should there be a subject line that identifies the account or file associated with the correspondence; should there be a line linking this message to another (*In reply to*)?
- Salutation—How does one address the recipient; what titles, greetings, and honorifics are preferred; how does one manage the problem of unknown gender; does one address men and women recipients differently?

- Body Text—What is the preferred form of indentation and paragraph separation; are there barriers against bullets, side headings, or other structured forms?
- Complimentary Closing—What polite phrase is typically used before the sender's signature; are special meanings associated with different closings?
- Signature/ID—How should the senders identify themselves; how are the printed and hand-written signatures alike and different; are there rules for including one's job position or university degrees in the signature?
- Reference Initials—Is it appropriate to identify the author and typist with initials; does the recipient include other codes for identifying responsibility?
- Attachment ID, Page Numbers, and Other Documentation—Is it customary to number pages on a letter that exceeds a page; are there conventions for items that appear after the signature or in the footer to help file and manage the document, such as version numbers, project numbers, authorization codes, reviewers/censor's codes?
- Outside (Envelope) Address—What is the precise sequence of company, person, street address, postal code, and so forth? (Note: An error here can frustrate the automated mail processing system in that country, adding one or several days' delay.)

This list should illustrate how subtle and complex it is to localize just the format of the letter. Consider these representative samples of the many subtle variations in expected format:

France Sample:

Edmond H. Weiss　　　　　　　M. Jean Louis
Fordham Business School　　　　Director of Training
113 West 60 Street　　　　　　　DeGaulle Ltd.
New York, New York　　　　　　Morne Jaloux Place
10023 USA　　　　　　　　　　6000 Paris

New York 15 August 2004

Sir,

Texttexttexttext texttexttexttext texttexttexttext texttexttexttext texttexttexttext texttexttexttext texttexttexttext.

Texttexttexttext texttexttexttext texttexttexttext texttexttexttext texttexttexttext texttexttexttext texttexttexttext.

Coordinator of Intercultural Program
Edmond H. Weiss

Saudi Arabia Sample (both correspondents are Muslims):

Youssef Al-Wadi   15 August 2004
Madina Conference Center
112 Cadde-ul sehr, Madina
Kingdom of Saudi Arabia

Bismillahirrahmanirrahim
Esselamun aleykum ve
rahmetulla

Dear Brother,

Texttexttexttext texttexttexttext texttexttexttext texttexttexttext
texttexttexttext texttexttexttext texttexttexttext texttexttexttext
texttexttexttext texttexttexttext texttexttexttext. Texttexttexttext
texttexttexttext texttexttexttext texttexttexttext texttexttexttext
texttexttexttext texttexttexttext texttexttexttext texttexttexttext
texttexttexttext texttexttexttext.

Texttexttexttext texttexttexttext texttexttexttext texttexttexttext
texttexttexttext texttexttexttext texttexttexttext. Texttexttexttext
texttexttexttext texttexttexttext texttexttexttext texttexttexttext
texttexttexttext texttexttexttext texttexttexttext.

Esselamun aleykum ve rahmetulla

Ahmet Houri
Global Training Systems
New York, United States of America

Japan Sample:

August 15, 2004

Dr. Taskashi Kobyasha
Manager of Planning
Tokyo Business
Development Council
15-17 Ginza 9 chome
Chuo-ku Tokyo 104

Dr. Edmond Weiss
President
Crown Point
Communications
2000 Cooper Road
Crown Point,
New Jersey 03001

Dear Dr. Kobyasha:
Texttexttexttext texttexttexttext texttexttexttext.

Texttexttexttext texttexttexttext texttexttexttext texttexttexttext texttexttexttext texttexttexttext texttexttexttext texttexttexttext texttexttexttext texttexttexttext texttexttexttext. Texttexttexttext texttexttexttext texttexttexttext texttexttexttext texttexttexttext texttexttexttext texttexttexttext texttexttexttext texttexttexttext texttexttexttext.

Sincerely yours,
Edmond H. Weiss
President

Tactic 51: Emulate the Receiver's Opening Paragraph and Customary Closing

American business communication consultants agree on most things but not on how to begin a business letter. Specifically, the most divisive question is how to start the presentation of bad news. (Nearly everyone has more trouble writing bad news correspondence than good news.) The first sentence or two of a bad news letter is usually called the "buffer" because its purported function is to soften the blow or ameliorate the pain in the message. Everyone who has ever been turned down for a job, loan, or favor has seen a buffer:

- Thank you for submitting your excellent resume ...
- We read your application with great interest ...
- Thank you for your generous offer to ...

Buffers are a noble idea, an antidote for the blunt, insensitive way that some people write. After decades of their use, however, some of us have come to challenge their efficacy, especially when they are couched in clichés and stock phrases. In other words, the goal of showing concern for the recipient of bad news is ill served by hackneyed language that suggests a lack a genuine interest in the recipient of the bad news.

The buffer battle rages on, however. Most Americans are simply afraid of beginning a letter by saying: *We hired someone else for the Coordinator's position.* And those writers are somewhat better prepared to communicate in the local letter styles of other countries. With few exceptions, every country's letter culture expects some ritual expression of feeling or some philosophical observation in the opening paragraph. (I recently received an e-mail from Pakistan that began: *I hope you will be safe and sound.*) Those E1s who are eager to get directly to their actual business (as I am when I have bad news to deliver) must restrain themselves and learn the appropriate local etiquette.

There are several ritualized openings, depending on the country. Most fit into these categories:

- Solicitation of the recipient's well-being (Careful: In some countries it is taboo to inquire about the recipient's family, especially a man's wife)
- Grateful recollection of past meetings, especially of the last visit to the recipient's country

- Reflection on the changing of the seasons, or of a current holiday or festival, or the anniversary of a historically significant event
- Comments on the beauties of nature, especially in the recipient's homeland at this time of year
- Homage to the importance or accomplishments of the recipient, the recipient's company or government or country
- Philosophical or religious commentary, including proverbs or quotes from appropriate scriptures or literature

The options for concluding are fewer, but they, too, are ritualized. Most letters end with an indication of what comes next, if anything. In some countries, however, it is bad form to mention future meetings or events without a humble disclaimer acknowledging divine will.

Although there may come a day when casual e-mail will supplant this demonstration of politesse, for now, one of the central chores for those somewhat rough-hewn North Americans who wish to localize their letters for the rest of the world is to learn how to pay a compliment, speak sincerely of nature's beauty, or offer a philosophical insight.

Tactic 52: Emulate the Receiver's Content Restrictions

Various countries also have different traditions regarding the content of letters. In some places, for example, the prices of goods and services should NOT be documented in writing, since that would foreclose the eventual spoken negotiation and bargaining process. EIs should learn the negotiation cultures in the recipient's country to determine whether hard numbers, black on white, would help or hinder the process. Such research should be in-depth and country-specific. Two works that provide a broad framework for this preparation are Dean Foster's *Bargaining across Borders* and Jeffrey Curry's *A Short Course in International Negotiating*.

Some countries, notably Mexico, expect a letter to be filled with personal information and expressions of sentiment, whereas others, including Switzerland, want only hard, cold facts committed in writing. Too much intimacy in the letter might suggest a biased business decision. As already noted, certain favored topics, such as references to the seasons, recur in the letters of certain countries, whereas other topics—even certain words—are taboo. To repeat an extremely sensitive point, in some countries one is thanked for asking about the well-being of the recipient's family members; in others, Saudi Arabia, for example, the very word *wife* will provoke an angry response.

Note that national borders and the legitimacy of governments are in dispute throughout the world, making it an unspeakable blunder to take the wrong side through one's choice of words. For example, Microsoft Corporation referred to Taiwan as a "country" in one of its setup utilities and alienated the People's Republic of China. Similarly, in a graphical representation of the world map it resolved the Kashmir conflict by making its one pixel the same color as that of one of the disputant countries (India and Pakistan). Both of these lapses, small to Western eyes, were serious enough problems to warrant correction in the next version of the software.

Complicating matters, in many parts of the world there is a so-called disconnect between what everyone knows and what one is permitted to speak or write. For instance, one government may officially not recognize another, but may secretly have diplomatic and business relationships. If E1's business communication is part of that unspoken dynamic, it limits what may be written and forces E1s to use certain oblique, almost obfuscating language, like calling an embassy an "interest center" or "trade delegation." Currently, for example, the outsourcing of American technical and administrative jobs to India and China has become a politically sensitive topic. Not surprisingly, then, the companies that broker and provide these services are using names and descriptions that give no clue to what they do.

Moreover, in many cultures business is not really conducted in writing at all. These so-called high-context cultures rely more on unexpressed understandings than written agreements. Some countries have unofficial or secret political and business relationships, in which there is a separate version of the truth for public and private consumption. In addition, there are clandestine cultures in which business is actually conducted through exchange of favors, purchase of influence, and political manipulation, in which bids and contracts are just for show.

We should note that part of cultural sensitivity lies in refraining from characterizing these practices as dishonest or evil. One person's bribe is another's sales commission or broker's fee. In the United States, for example, bribes to government officials are usually in the form of campaign contributions. And there are times when progress can be made only in secret because of overwhelming political or ethnic pressures.

Remember that writing is a kind of frozen or captured speech, which in many cases is nearly permanent. Two persons may nullify one another's recollection of what was spoken in a negotiation, but hard copy is difficult to deny. For that reason, much international correspondence and documentation must be written in a code—if not in outright falsehoods. Those who are uncomfortable with these ground rules may elect to resign from the game.

What about E-mail?

Before the mid-1990s, e-mail systems tended to be within companies or single-purpose networks. E-mail messages were usually short, limited to plain text (sometimes all upper case), and incidental to the many other forms of business and corporate communication. Even when that changed, though, when everyone had learned the syntax of the @ sign, the uses of email were still circumscribed: generally, two- or three-sentence texts resembling the short messages we had only recently learned to leave on telephone answering machines.

By the end of the twentieth century, however, those who taught and studied business communication found e-mail increasingly interesting and worrisome. On the one hand, people were writing again; professionals who previously did all their communicating on the telephone, who rarely sent a memo or wrote a letter, increasingly spent a good part of each day writing and reading. On the other hand, the rough and reckless e-mail approach to writing—disregard for standard spelling, grammar, capitalization, or punctuation, (along with cryptic abbreviations and acronyms like BTW)—filled the stewards of proper English with alarm.

E-mail is more than a channel or medium or technology. It is a communication culture of its own, offering global interaction at nearly the speed of light, while discounting the stylized, mannered, formal culture of traditional professional communication. Although recent technology makes available every kind of formatted text and graphical layout, even though a contemporary e-mail message can contain not only dynamic links to changing data but also animated graphical presentations of those changes, most e-mail is still rough and reckless plain text, much of it written without the use of the <SHIFT> key.

It avails English teachers and communication consultants little to rail against this decline. We can warn our clients that e-mail needs to be reread, edited, and refined before it is sent; we can cite research showing that most of the substandard English in e-mails works against the professional interests of the senders. But most e-mail users are unimpressed with these arguments. They are not only unapologetic but insurgent; they hold that the quick, no-frills way of communicating is inherently better than the polite alternatives.

In any case, those who use e-mail to pursue serious professional and business objectives—as opposed to casual, friendly exchanges—should be mindful of certain rules of structure and etiquette that affect the reliability of the medium. For example,

- Date and Time can be expressed in several forms, but, as mentioned before, certain American dating conventions produce anomalous results. (2/7/09 is a winter day in New York and a summer one in Germany.) Also, international e-mails should include not only the local time of origin, but also GMT (Greenwich Mean Time, or Greenwich Meridian Time, also known as Universal Time). GMT is the local time in London but is not adjusted for Daylight Saving Time. It is five hours later than Eastern Standard Time in the United States.
- Subject Lines must be clear and complete enough to attract the attention of the reader. Only those who are new to e-mail open all their messages; most businesspeople and professionals delete unwanted and uninteresting messages before they read anything. Subject lines, therefore, must be substantive and interesting. Instead of *Meeting Update* write *Revised date for Project Launch or, better, Project Launch moved to 15 October.* Instead of *ISO Status* write *ISO registrars promise report by May.*
- Body text should contain short sentences and short paragraphs. When possible, lists and simple tables should replace paragraphs, and widely available ASCI symbols (>, =, #) should be used to serve as bullets and emphasis devices.
- Unsolicited sales material is never acceptable in international e-mails. For most Westerners "junk e-mail" or "spam" is an irritant, but in most of the world it is regarded as an unforgivable breach of business etiquette and will make further relationships impossible. One should always send a one- or two-sentence e-mail first, asking permission to send the longer sales material or business proposal.

Adapting E-mail for International Recipients

The question is whether e-mail culture is suitable for International English exchanges or whether, for example, it is better to attach a fully formatted, traditional letter to a one-line e-mail letter of transmittal. The answer is complicated by various stages of e-mail development and forms of e-mail culture in the many nations of the world. Those countries with a long tradition of letter writing, in which the art and craft of the letter are key parts of a young person's education, may be expected to find Western e-mail culture brusque and unsophisticated (like the cut-to-the-chase American sales presentation). Furthermore, those countries with a tradition of exceptional postal service (like the UK) or with an official government commitment to preserving correct diction and grammar (like France) might be put off by receiving important correspondence in the casual, plaintext e-mail style.

There is no obvious choice, however. Attitudes toward e-mail culture vary by industry as much as by country and, it appears, by the age of the correspondents. E-mail is also part of the phenomenon called *leapfrog* technology in which a country undergoing rapid economic or social development will skip one generation of technology and go directly to a more advanced one. Countries without a landline infrastructure, for example, may go directly to wireless phones and satellite TV systems. Similarly, countries without a tradition of business letter writing or formalized business speech may leap directly to the informal, casual e-mail approach.

The purpose of this discussion is not to assess the appropriateness of using e-mail. Nearly everyone in the word enjoys the breathtaking speed and convenience of this form of communication. Rather, the question is whether to use e-mail in the loose, energetic style that most people associate with the technology or, alternately, use it just as another channel to transmit either carefully globalized or expensively localized business messages. And, if the latter, how?

First, if research shows that the E2 recipient is comfortable with speedy, plaintext e-mail, does not find it inappropriately informal for the business at hand, it is still necessary to apply most of the tactics discussed in this text. Even though the style is informal and the text largely unformatted, the message is still being sent to someone who finds it at least somewhat difficult to read English and who may need to consult a bilingual dictionary. *Until* and *mind* are still hard words to translate; *I am waiting* is still harder to understand than *I wait; key player, put up with,* and *prewireless* are hard to look up. This means that, at the very least, an International English e-mail should be studied and edited before the writer hits the <Send> key.

If E1 decides to send a traditional letter, especially one localized to the format and content preferences of the recipient, there are still other questions:

- Are attachments safe and welcome? Does the recipient's e-mail system discourage attachments or even block them. Is the recipient's e-mail system fast enough to download larger attachments, without annoying the receiver and tying up the resources? Will the attachment travel reliably; that is, will the formatting and numbering be distorted by the several bounces of the document through the global communication network?
- Is it feasible to send formatted plain text? In the early days of computing, skillful programmers could generate clever graphics composed of thousands of the letter x and a few equal signs. To format plain text well takes ingenuity—after all, there are not even bullets. But a moment or two can make a string of uninviting characters far more accessible and readable.

The example that follows shows how small changes in plain text can make an e-mail far easier to read.

Unformatted Plain Text

Jack . . . The meeting went as planned. Audrey had three objections to the proposed date for the next conference—the conflict with IEEE convention, the short time to solicit and evaluate papers and presentations, the fact that we need a new printer since the company we used last year has raised its prices too high. We also agreed that the four programs at the conference would be Voice Command Recognition, Voice-Based Security Systems, Machine Translation of Arabic, Research & Development Priorities. Jan complained, by the way, that most of the presentations last year were just commercials for consultants and we would need better science and analysis this year.

Formatted Plain Text

```
=================================================
To: Jack
Subject: 2006 Speech Recognition Conference Planning
=================================================
OBJECTIONS TO DATE (Audrey)
>> The conflict with IEEE convention dates
>> The short time to solicit and evaluate papers and pre-
sentations
>> The need to secure a new printer
***(The company we used last year has raised its prices too
high.)***
```

```
OBJECTIONS TO CONTENT (Jan)
>> Most of the presentations last year were just commercials
for consultants
>> We would need better science and analysis this year


===============================================
Proposed Program
===============================================
o Voice Command Recognition
o Voice-Based Security Systems
o Machine Translation of Spoken Arabic
o Research & Development Priorities.
```

- Is it feasible to embed a fully formatted document based on SGML or XML (two of the most widely-used hypertext markup languages)? When attachments are a problem, and plain text is too limiting, the best course is to embed or insert a "marked-up" hypertext document in the e-mail panel. This process grows easier with each generation of word processing software and allows the senders to make as refined a letter as they wish. Again, the senders should be sure that there is no barrier to hypertext documents at the receiver's end, especially as more and more organizations are blocking potential computer viruses by disabling certain hypertext features.

Most business letters communicate a small, important objective in a key passage or two, which is then surrounded by mannerism, affectation, ritual, tradition, and even a bit of deception. Unfortunately, if this ornamental, content-free material surrounding the core content is handled badly—for example, if a title is wrong, if there is insufficient deference, or if the wrong holiday sentiment is expressed—the sender can fail to achieve the business objective. Informal e-mail culture may change this some day. Indeed, the coarse communication style nowadays associated with Instant Messages and cell phone "texting" may some day cause us to remember fondly the more polite and readable style of e-mails!
But not for a while.

Discussion Questions

- Do you currently send memos to your colleagues and associates? in what circumstances?
- How do you feel when you read the buffer of a bad news letter? Does it help?

- Are you comfortable writing buffers? paying compliments? commenting on the season?
- Do you receive more than an occasional business letter? in what circumstances?
- Do you reread and revise your e-mails before you send them? How much time do you spend on a typical email message? Is it enough?
- Have you ever been embarrassed by the substandard grammar and spelling in your e-mails?
- Have you ever judged an unknown person by the care or carelessness of his or her e-mails?

Sources and Resources

Angell, David, and Brent Heslop. *The Elements of E-Mail Style.* Reading, MA: Addison-Wesley, 1994.

Atkinson, Toby. *Merriam Webster's Guide to International Business Communication.* 2nd ed. Springfield, MA: Merriam-Webster, 1996.

Baron, Naomi S. *Alphabet to Email: How Written English Evolved and Where It's Heading.* London/New York: Routledge, 2000.

Business Netiquette International: http://www.bspage.com/1netiq/Netiq.html

Curry, Jeffrey. *A Short Course in International Negotiating.* New York: World Trade Press, 1999.

DeVries, Mary. *Internationally Yours: Writing and Communicating Successfully in Today's Global Marketplace.* New York: Houghton Mifflin, 1994.

Emily Post's Letter Writing Etiquette, 1922 (http://www.bartleby.com/95/28.html)

Foster, Dean. *Bargaining across Borders.* New York: McGraw-Hill, 1992.

Frank's Compulsive Guide to Postal Addresses (http://www.columbia.edu/kermit/postal.html)

Hall, Edward T., and Mildred Reed Hall. *Understanding Cultural Differences.* Yarmouth, ME: Intercultural Press, 1990.

ISO Standards for International E-mail Accessibility (http://www.nsrc.org/codes/country-codes.html)

Kaitlin, Sherwood. *A Beginner's Guide to Effective Email*: http://www.is.kiruna.se/english/emailguide/email.top.html

Kirsner, Scott. *The Elements of Email Style*: http://www.darwinmag.com/read/100101/ecosystem.html

Letter Etiquette: http://www.3mom.com/html/letter_etiquette.html

7

Principles of Cultural Adaptation

International English Style calls for an unusual sensitivity to the diverse cultures of the world, as well as some humility. Even those E1s who believe that they live in the most advanced civilization on earth must discipline themselves to keep such an attitude in check, avoiding the phrase or tone that suggests condescension toward those who communicate differently or use different criteria to assess truth or evaluate ideas. The objective of this chapter, therefore, is to explore some of the issues and controversies associated with intercultural communication and business transactions.

Was der Bauer nicht kennt . . .

There are at least two good reasons for adapting to the culture of E2 readers. First, it is the polite, civil thing to do; in some ways it is another application of the Golden Rule. Second, it is a necessary step in the process of doing business abroad. The first reason may be considered idealistic, humanitarian, and the second is just enlightened self-interest. Consider the German proverb: *Was der Bauer nicht kennt, das frisst er nicht.* (What the farmer doesn't know, he can't eat.) Notice that, in this conception, the verb *frisst* [eats] is the term used in German for how animals eat.

Those of us who lived through the second half of the twentieth century are sometimes amused at the recent cosmopolitanism of American business, the eagerness of American business professionals to learn the customs and cultures of other nations. Fifty years ago, such interests were regarded with suspicion, and the advocates for improved communication between, say, the United States and the People's Republic of China were frequently condemned and marginalized. Today, however, countless books and in-flight magazines are filled with tips on how to avoid offending businesspeople in other countries. These days one finds more than a few multiculturalists at the Chamber of Commerce meetings. Even so, I notice that DisneyWorld vendors still sell a yin-yang symbol with mouse ears!

It is fascinating that so many utterly practical people are fascinated with the elusive, even esoteric construct of *culture*. To simplify this discussion, we can define culture as a system of beliefs, biases, and expectations with which people persistently interpret and absorb their environment. This is an oversimplification but adequate for our purpose. Cultural anthropology teaches us that everyone, at all times, processes the world through lenses that shape and distort their perceptions. For those who believe that perception IS reality, of course, the word "distort" is inappropriate. Even very young infants stop producing the sounds that are not part of their language and stop hearing differences between sounds that are perceived differently in other languages but not their own.

In business, the process of cultural education—sometimes called diversity training—tries to make us aware of the characteristic ways our own lenses work, the difference between hard data and the cultural interpretation of that data. We learn that scores of practical business situations and the evaluative language associated with them are culturally charged. What constitutes being *late?* Is *disagreement* a sign of *disrespect?* Can a woman *lead* a team of men? Should contracts be precise or *flexible?*

Those who attend these courses and seminars learn that the answer to all these questions is supposed to become, through training, the same: It depends. Multiculturalists urge us to manage our own preferences and prejudices, to control our initial reactions and suspend judgment about others' behavior. This process may not come easily to people who have been taught to make quick decisions and act on consistent principles.

But everyone, even those who cannot see the world through any lenses other than those of their own culture and religion, can be taught at least to tolerate other cultures long enough to make a deal.

Interestingly, effective international and intercultural communication requires, above all else, the strategy first enunciated by Aristotle in the *Rhetoric:* adaptation to one's audience, modifying one's material so that it includes more of what interests and engages the receiver of the message than the sender. And, equally interesting, many critics of this multicultural approach to business echo the same objections that Plato once raised about rhetoric: that it is more meretricious than respectful, that it is a form of condescension toward one's audience based on the arrogant notion that people can be persuaded and motivated by simple flattery and manipulation of their emotions.

This dispute between philosophy (nowadays science) and rhetoric is both classic and classical. For as long as people have thought seriously about communication, there have been those who believed that any self-conscious packaging of information designed to attract and please the audience is merely a sophisticated form of deception. More than a few people have always believed that the professional communicator (sophist in ancient Greece, Press Secretary today) is someone whose main skill is to lie with impunity. At the same time, there has been the rhetorical side of the argument—the belief that communication simply cannot occur at all unless the sender (rhetor) fits the language, themes, sequence, and pace to the audience, changing these things when the audience changes. For a discussion of this debate, see Weiss (1995).

Like all the best debates, this debate is likely to remain unresolved forever. In certain epochs, one side will be in intellectual ascendance, while the other side is characterized as old-fashioned or reactionary. Currently, the preponderance of opinion favors the rhetorical approach in international business communication, that is, adaptation by the sender to the receiver. What became apparent in the 1980s was that, among countries that wanted to do business globally, especially in the Far East, those countries that studied and respected the cultures of others gained a marked competitive advantage. Such small tactics as learning a country's religious or historical holidays and commenting on a recent one in the opening of a business letter seemed to matter more than one would have predicted.

In contrast, countries and companies that took a one-size-fits-all approach to marketing and product design fared badly. No Japanese car aimed at European or North American markets ever arrived with the steering wheel on the wrong side; the United States, however, persisted in sending cars with left-side steering wheels to Japan and then complained that their products were being unfairly restricted.

The position of a steering wheel is an example of what might be called a cultural *convention*, an arbitrary choice made long ago and still perceived as an arbitrary choice. It is doubtful that anyone would argue for the superiority of left- versus right-side drive. Yet, after a long time it becomes so deeply ingrained that changing it would distress whole populations. For example, London intersections have arrows and warnings painted onto the streets advising the millions of visitors from countries where cars drive on the right side to look the other way before crossing. Following the signs requires a great exertion of will.

Some aspects of culture, however, including some that began as arbitrary conventions—such as putting on or taking off one's hat in certain religious circumstances—rise to the level of what might be called values. What seem like small and inconsequential matters to persons in one culture—like putting someone's business card into your wallet and then into your back pocket—may be perceived as insulting or uncivilized to persons in another. The rationale behind much of today's thinking in intercultural communication, it would seem, is avoiding offense. Thus, even the suggestion that someone's valued traditions began as arbitrary conventions, even though it is demonstrably true, would violate the etiquette of international business communication.

For the most part, then, the following section suggests tactics for ensuring that International English documents do not anger, distract, or annoy the intended recipients. Taking a rhetorical approach, the method currently in favor, the tactics indicate how the senders can first become sensitized to their own cultural peculiarities and then modify them to more resemble the receiver's expectations. Implicit in this presentation is the idea that the alternate view also deserves attention—the antirhetorical notion that urges us to communicate well from within our own culture rather than trying to emulate the superficial aspects of the other's culture. More will be said on this matter at the end of the chapter.

Tactic 53: Be Extremely Polite and Formal

Among the traits most admired in American business culture are its directness, lack of complicated etiquette, and efficient use of time and resources. The expression *Let's cut to the chase* embodies the American's distaste for formalities, cautious buildups, and unnecessary background or context. *What's the bottom line?* embodies a simple, clear set of values in which what directly affects the outcome or profit matters, whereas everything else is *fun and games*. And *Always be closing!* is the motto of a businessperson who has no time to waste and other prospects to convert.

This robust, energetic, and efficient approach to business, though admired and imitated in many places, is viewed as uncouth, immature, and impolite in others. The fresh, vital, informal style of many American businesspeople is likely to appear rude in those countries that prefer a slower, more gradual process of introduction and collaboration. Many E1 documents, especially American business correspondence, are just too informal for other countries. International documents travel better if they are exceedingly polite and formal. Unfortunately, however, those writers who are used to an informal style typically misinterpret what is meant by "formal" and lapse instead into a stiff, bureaucratic, pseudolegalistic style that no one wants to read. (It is a mistake to call this kind of writing "legalese"; inasmuch as good legal writing is clear and accessible.)

By formal style is meant:

- No first names or other familiarities (My MBA students frequently refer to the authors of books and articles by their first names! As though they were friends.)
- No contractions (like *don't*) or popular acronyms or shortened forms (like *ASAP* or *24/7*)
- No non-standard punctuation (like linking two sentences with a comma or dash) or spelling (like *nite*)
- No colloquialisms or slang (like *dump* or *non-starter*)

    Before:
        Our guys were hoping to get some face time with your quality people before we button up the proposal.
    After:
        Our engineering team wants to meet with your quality assurance group, before we complete the proposal.

Formal communication also means strict enforcement of grammar and syntax, including the avoidance of sentence fragments, such as *As though they were friends* in the previous passage. When a competent author writes a sentence fragment on purpose, the string of words is called an elliptical sentence—a deliberately incomplete sentence that is nevertheless clear because everyone can deduce the missing words. The fragment above stands for: *My students act as though the authors were their friends.* Again, even though students are usually corrected for writing sentence fragments, and even though Microsoft Word flags them as errors, professional writers use these constructions all the time. But they have no place in formal writing, as one might also argue for sentences beginning with *but.* And they will probably be perceived as an error by the many E2 readers who know the rules of sentence formation.

As mentioned in the section on international correspondence, E1s should also learn some correspondence etiquette suitable for the persons receiving the message. In particular, each country has traditional ways of beginning and ending letters and presentations. E1s should honor these traditions, even when they seem alien, inappropriate, inefficient, or too fancy for a business exchange. This kind of impatient, bristling attitude is representative of the cultural intolerance that students of intercultural communication are expected to contain and suppress.

Tactic 54: Assess Other Cultures without Stereotyping

Inherent in the last discussion was the implication that certain countries are more mannered, elegant, and even more publicly religious than Americans. At the same time, the passage asserts directly that a large proportion of American businesspeople are seen as arrogant, coarse, provincial, and insensitive in their communication style. The problem with any attempt to describe cultural differences is that, first, like any generalizations they are imprecise and often shallow, and, second, that they use descriptive language that inherently favors one set of phenomena over the other. The first problem, misleading generalizations, can be overcome by good research and cautious interpretation of the results. The second problem, prejudicial language, is more resistant to solution.

When we describe cultures and countries and when we create categories and dimensions to differentiate one from the other, we tend to use words that have a value charge, words that communicate the preferences of the observer's culture. In more technical terms, our descriptive vocabulary is *stereotypical,* not *archetypical* (for an extended discussion of this idea, see Foster, 1992). So, for example, when Geert Hofstede

(1997) states that the United States and the UK are more "individualistic" and that Korea and Japan are more "collectivistic," he has chosen terms that are fraught with evaluative meaning to a Western reader. The issue is not whether he is correct; the many researchers who have replicated and refined Hofstede's research confirm the reliability of the Individualism-Collectivism dimension. Rather, the issue is that the word "individualistic" has a very salutary sound in most Western ears, whereas "collectivistic" is associated with Soviet-style communism and other notions that Westerners have been taught to distrust or abjure.

Naturally, we can expect almost every E1 already to be cautious of terms that grow out of negative racial or national stereotypes and prejudices. Although most educated people are prudent enough not to express any ethnic or national prejudice they may have, fewer realize that even complimentary and flattering stereotypes are also objectionable. If *individualistic* is a favorable term in your vocabulary, then referring to a nation by that term may be a prejudicial stereotype. Even referring to a particular nation or ethnic group as industrious, or honest, or intellectual is also a form of arrogance or condescension.

In recent years, businesspeople and business students have been drawn to excellent compendiums, such as the delightfully-named *Kiss, Bow, or Shake Hands* (Morrison et al., 1994), in which the authors offer a short readable chapter on the culture, customs, and selected business practices in sixty countries. The goal of the book is to teach its readers, especially its American business readers, to avoid offense: to steer clear of certain conversational topics in Turkey, to handle business cards with suitable appreciation in China, to be unamazed if, in certain countries, the person you are meeting with invites a visiting family member to join you. One reason for the popularity of such books is that they reduce the subtleties of culture to simple lists. In Morrison et al.'s work, each chapter is a small briefing book on how to comport oneself abroad. And there is no doubt that the information is generally sound. Consider this excerpt from the chapter on the United States:

- In negotiations, points are made by the accumulation of facts. These are sometimes biased by faith in the ideologies of democracy, capitalism, and consumerism, but seldom by the subjective feelings of the participants. (p. 406)
- Most business people have business cards, but these cards are not exchanged unless you want to contact the person later. (p. 408)

- When staying in a U.S. home, you will probably be expected to help out around the house by making your bed, helping to clear the dishes after a meal, and so forth. (p. 411)

Obviously, these observations are generally correct, but are there enough exceptions and special situations to make them unreliable for a person without experience in the United States. And if Americans see so many exceptions to their own cultural generalizations, how would Italians react to the claim, in the same book, that they are open to information but rarely change their opinions? (p. 198)

As indicated earlier, the current thinking on intercultural communication is that everyone should learn these preferences and taboos, either from extended research or from small chapters in business guides, and should reflect what they have learned in writing, speech, and general behavior. But this leads to a philosophical question:

> Can one assess the cultures of other nations or groups without, at the same time, descending into shallow stereotypes? Is the application of tendencies and trends to individuals not only bad statistics but bad behavior?

There may come a day when the Internet blurs and blends many of these differences; there may even come a day when the *Gastfreundschaft* tradition will return—when hosts do everything to make their foreign guests feel comfortable. In the meanwhile, we should keep trying to adapt to the cultures of the people whose business we want, even at the risk of getting it wrong and even at the risk of appearing tolerant, an irritating attitude that suggests feelings of superiority. Only the more powerful of two parties is in a position to tolerate the other.

Tactic 55: Localize Radically

Generally, all the tactics in this text are meant to remove burdens, distractions, and difficulties from international documents. In this effort, they support globalization and culture-free communication, and the elimination of anything that makes it peculiar to one culture or reader group at the expense of others.

But no document is truly ready for E2 readers until a reliable cultural adviser has reviewed it. This reviewer should be a representative of *the intended recipient nation or community*, and not merely a student of that country's culture. Such a person can alert the writers not only to minor errors and omissions in the tactics described in this text, but also to subtle and important cultural irritants. What Richard Brislin (1993) calls well-meaning clashes—trying to be polite but offending instead—are surprisingly common in intercultural exchanges. Thus, hiring a consultant or adviser with the appropriate cultural sensitivities may be the only reliable way to forestall a grave misunderstanding, and therefore will be worth the cost.

Ultimately, editing a document for ease and clarity, removing its unnecessary difficulties and cultural peculiarities, is much easier than adapting it to local expectations, adding elements that will make it more familiar, meaningful, and engaging to your readers. In *International Technical Communication,* Nancy Hoft calls this "radical localization."

The effort needed to research the culture of our readers, as well as the cost of acquiring cultural informants, may seem high at first, but in a world of global commerce, it is a sound investment. For example, consider William Horton's survey of the differing cultural effects of color as shown below.

Culture	Red	Yellow	Green	Blue
Europe/West	Danger	Caution Cowardice	Safe Sour	Masculine Sweet Calm Authority
Japanese	Anger Danger	Grace-nobility Childhood-gaiety	Future Youthful-energy	Villainy
Arabic		Happiness Prosperity	Fertility-strength	Virtue, faith, truth
Chinese	Joy-festivity	Honor Royalty		

Source: Horton, William, *Illustrating Computer User Documentation*, New York, Wiley, 1991, p. 213.

Having collected this information, we may ask: Now what? If E1's letterhead is in a color with unpleasant associations for the recipient (red in Japan, say), should the sender change it? Should E1 globalize, by removing all colors, or localize by choosing a color better liked by the recipient?

Tactic 56: Define Your Graphics Strategy

The chapter on reducing burdens recommended that EIs replace paragraphs with tables and diagrams. Part of localization, however, is researching the local disposition toward various forms of pictorial representation.

Some observers, like Edward Tufte (1990, p. 10), argue that "principles of information design are universal—like mathematics—and are not tied to unique features of a particular language or culture." Others, like Charles Kostelnick (1995), suggest that, although one could aim for a global, culture-free approach to graphical design, one might also choose to adapt to local cultures. The alternatives appear below.

	Global (modern)	Culture-focused (post-modern)
Design assumptions	Images can be simplified and homogenized to make them accessible to diverse audiences	Something is lost in simplification, or the generic images are culturally freighted
Design goals	Systemization, conventions & standards; generic forms erase cultural differences	Design must be adapted to cultural context, partly by invoking familiar conventions
Modes of reception	Universality of visual language is certified by perceptual psychology and empirical research	Users interpretations create meaning; visual language is learned experience

Source: "Cultural Adaptation and Information Design: Two Contrasting Views," *IEEE Transactions on Professional Communication* (1995) 182-195.

Although this framework may seem academic at first, it has a number of direct practical implications, especially relating to the pictorial representation of homes, workplaces, and the people in them. It also reminds us that people in diverse cultures see things differently and may have to be taught to recognize even photographs of familiar places and people.

Tactic 57: Consider Hall's Context Continuum

What could be more obviously true than the claim that good writing is clear and unambiguous? Who could argue with the idea that the more precisely we capture information in writing, the more documentation we have for our conversations and agreements, the better? Who could possibly prefer an incomplete or vague contract to a complete and specific one? The answer is that, in many parts of the world, businesspeople want things to be undocumented, prefer understandings to be vague (flexible), and put more faith in what the parties "understood" than in what was either said or written.

As an American writer and editor, one of the hardest concepts for me to grasp is Edward Hall's Context Continuum with its graduated distinction between high-context and low-context communication cultures. (Hall's *Beyond Culture*, 1981, is required reading for students of intercultural communication.) According to Hall, national communication cultures can be arrayed from

> **High-Context** cultures, where the written message is less important than the constellation of understandings—often unexpressed—between the sender and receiver, to
> **Low-Context** cultures, which rely on detailed, unambiguous messages

The following list shows, according to Hall's research, a ranking of major world cultures on a scale from high-context to low-context:

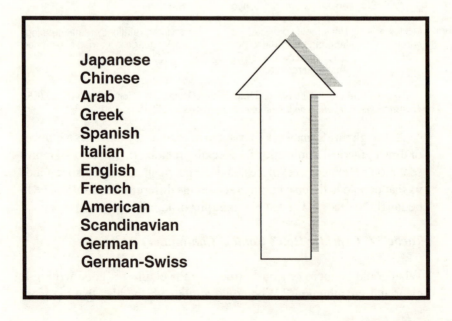

Japanese
Chinese
Arab
Greek
Spanish
Italian
English
French
American
Scandinavian
German
German-Swiss

These differences in communication behavior are great enough to cause significant misunderstandings. In a high-context negotiation, the parties will seem to agree with each other while somehow understanding that they disagree. The agreeable language is meant to avoid conflict or embarrassment. In a low-context negotiation, what people "understand" will be superseded by what actually appears, black on white, in the written papers. In a low-context culture, vaguely written forecasts are indicative of either fuzzy thinking or an unwillingness to commit; in a high-context culture, deliberate ambiguity and imprecision is a sign of maturity, a humble appreciation of the impossibility of predicting the future. Moreover, in a high-context culture, people who are "pretending" to know the future will be understood to be pretending.

For those of us who consult and teach about writing exclusively in low-context countries, the goal is clear: help students and clients to write simple, direct, clear, unambiguous facts and procedures, along with readable, logical arguments and interpretations. We counsel people to say exactly what they mean, to be as forthright and truthful as circumstances permit, and then we scold them for careless or deliberate obfuscation. The problem for communicators and consultants arises when the communication is between cultures far apart on Hall's continuum.

How can we prepare EIs for the fact that, when, for example, they ask a Korean the wrong question, the Korean will deduce the question they meant to ask and answer that one instead? Contrast this with the way American lawyers prepare witnesses to answer only the question asked, nothing more, regardless of the interrogator's clear meaning. (I once asked a client whether he could find the error in a certain document; he answered, "Yes.")

Issues of Philosophy and "Hypernorms"

International communication occasionally presents us with problems that are less a matter of technique than of philosophy. As I indicated at the beginning of this chapter, the ancient debate about whether to adapt to the other culture's expectations is never likely to be resolved and the currently favored position is that the sender should do all the adapting, not the host or recipient. More precisely, in business situations this usually means that the needier of the parties, the one with the most to gain, adapts to the demands and expectations of the other. In plainer terms still, the buyer adapts to the seller in a seller's market and vice versa. For example, when I ask MBA students whether they would eat a repulsive food served by their foreign customer so as to avoid jeopardizing a business deal, they usually answer: It depends on how much money is involved.

Many EIs may elect to buck the trend, as it were, and insist that some ways of communicating are inherently better than others, no matter which side prefers them. Again, this is an unfashionable position these days, but it can still be argued persuasively in specific contexts. What are the philosophical controversies inherent in international business communication, and what are the various stances one may take?

First, is it not possible that the traditional principles of business and professional communication—clarity, directness, simplicity—are in some sense universal? Or are they, as a scholar at the East-West Center chided me, merely "masculine" with "low context"? Would not the world be a better place if all persons with worthwhile ideas learned the craft of getting and holding attention and presenting a case forcefully? Or is there something aggressive, even amoral, in the Western communication teacher's preoccupation with effectiveness as the main criterion for judging communication competence? (For a chilling assessment of this question, see Katz, 1992.)

Is perfectly reliable, unambiguous communication across cultures and languages either feasible or desirable? Furthermore, if it can be achieved only by putting aside carefully edited natural English and replacing it with a kind of high-tech pidgin like Simplified English, then who wants it? Obviously, no professional business or technical writers want to work within such strictures. And certainly no advertising copywriters or public relations specialists would be content to prepare ads or releases with no *ing*-verbals in them. Worse, what satisfaction can there be for those people who work in ideas, whose interaction is through concepts and constructs, whose contribution is to perceive and communicate in well-made passages such things as subtle variations from conventional wisdom, interesting tradeoffs, new interpretations of old data—all those for whom there should never be an impediment to starting a sentence with *until* or *unless?*

Is it appropriate and ethical for those who study intercultural communication to lend their insights and research to the pursuit of amoral or immoral business objectives? Since much of the current emphasis on global communication is motivated not by liberal or humanitarian impulses but by the crassest of business motives, should scholars and consultants be worried that their services may be used to find, for example, better ways of selling cigarettes in countries that still allow it?

Are intercultural communication experts responsible when their research and insights are used to exploit persons in other countries and cultures to their measurable disadvantage?

Finally, in this postmodern and multiculturalist era, when managers are studying anthropology and reading Michel Foucault, *must we believe that all attempts at cultural conversion—imposition of the North American culture of clear, direct, unornamented writing, for example—are automatically immoral or even ineffective?* Is it not possible that nearly everyone in the world would benefit from learning to write in a leaner, more economical style, or that there might be immense global economies in eliminating the stylistic affectations of business letters?

Is not tolerance the most subtle form of intolerance and condescension? If the client is never wrong and if the local culture is always to be respected, are we not asked to overlook beliefs and behaviors that we judge to be immoral, superstitious, or unproductive? Are we obliged, for example, to believe in luck and magic, to avoid astrologically ill-favored dates for meetings, and to avoid using certain portentous numbers and words in the names of products?

The alternative to accepting all cultures and never challenging their legitimacy is to invoke a higher principle, a rule that can adjudicate between two cultures and find one of them inferior. Such a rule might be called a hypernorm, a precept that authorizes someone to violate a local rule or dispute a local expectation. (*Hypernorm* is a term coined by Thomas Donaldson, 1996.) Multiculturalists will generally dispute that there can be such a hypernorm, especially if it is based on someone's culturally-peculiar notion of divine law or absolute principles—a process that has been used more than once in history to justify the suppression of one nation by another. To illustrate how prickly this debate can be, consider the following remarks by Madeleine Albright, a modernist feminist, made when she was U.S. Secretary of State in 1997:

> We're opposed to their approach to human rights, to their despicable treatment of women and children, and their lack of respect for human dignity.

Albright was speaking about Afghanistan's Taliban regime and today, especially after 2001, most Westerners and many in Muslim countries would not object to the intolerant tone of her remarks. Except that the provocative columnist Crispin Sartwell did (1997):

> I am not sure whether a culture in which women are draped in burqas and are not allowed on the streets except for specific reasons respects

human dignity less than a culture in which women are dressed in g-strings and paid to dance on tables.

Indeed, I have heard feminists argue both positions: that women should be allowed to honor whatever religious traditions they choose and that women should not be oppressed by the religious traditions they happen to have been born to. The key to resolving the debate, however, is the word *choose*. Sartwell continues, "We have to talk to the women involved and try to figure out who feels free, if anyone."

Donaldson, in his elaboration on hypernorms, makes the same point: Are we obliged to respect a cultural rule when the members of the community have no choice in accepting or changing the rule or even feel oppressed by it? In this neomodernistic view, culture is a kind of contract, and its validity derives from informed consent. This viewpoint, reasonable on its surface, is hard to apply, however. Often, the adherents of religious and political orthodoxies do not believe they have any choice but to serve those orthodoxies and, by implication, to frustrate or destroy any people or forces that challenge or threaten those orthodoxies. As of this writing, the proportion of the world's population in the grip of such thinking seems to be increasing—which is hardly what the philosophers of the Enlightenment would have predicted.

Even so, I am sympathetic to Donaldson's arguments, perhaps because my own cultural upbringing characterizes the relationship between God and humankind as a contract, with obligations on both sides. In any case, although I nearly always adapt to my audience, there are times when I will choose to do things my own way, not the recipient's way, for reasons of principle that overwhelm the attractiveness of making a deal. It may seem far-fetched to suggest that controversies over writing style rise to the same level of ethical significance as controversies over, say, the rights of women, but, in my experience, *many questions of ethics are in fact matters of language*, and many stylistic practices reflect deeply embedded attitudes about truth and fairness.

What are some of the principles I am reluctant to modify for business reasons?

- I will never make a clear passage ambiguous because the recipient prefers it that way.
- I will never revise a document that is easy to read to make it more difficult to read because the recipient finds it unimpressive.
- I will not organize my business or professional life according to

superstitious fortune-telling systems or groundless notions that certain numbers, days, or months are "bad luck." (A superstition is a false causal connection.)

- I will never consciously do anything that damages the power and precision of the English language, which I regard as a priceless legacy.

Stating my refusals in hypernorm terms, I do not believe that anyone, given the requisite information and freedom to decide, would prefer unreadable, ambiguous texts. I refuse to believe that, once taught the science and freed to choose, people would prefer baseless cosmologies and numerologies to good physics, chemistry, and biology. And, finally, I choose to be a steward of the English language—not resisting all changes but doing what I can to ensure that the changes are for the better and do not devalue this treasure.

These occasional refusals to adapt to the audience—possibly nothing more than my own cultural biases—are at variance with the currently popular approach to international business communication, which is to emulate the style and satisfy the expectations of the recipient whenever possible. I cannot expect most people, especially those whose goal is a short-term profit, to share my philosophical concerns.

But I can expect E1s who communicate with E2s to be thoughtful about these controversies. Indeed, a kit of reliable writing tactics and a few moments of thoughtfulness (plus a dollop of imagination) are all most people need to write in an effective International English Style.

Discussion Questions

- Have you ever worked for more than a few days in a foreign country where English was spoken widely as a second language? What was most challenging about the experience?
- Have you ever worked for more than a few days in a foreign country where very few people spoke English? What was most challenging about the experience?
- If you were going to learn another language, which would it be? Why? How would you go about learning it?
- Have you experienced an embarrassment because of a well-meant cultural blunder? How did you handle it?
- Have you ever experienced a foreign business practice that made you uncomfortable? What, if anything, did you do about it?
- Are there some things you would never do to make a business deal? Are you sure? You mean the customer is not *always* right?

Sources and Resources

Axtell, Roger E. *Do's and Taboos around the World.* New York: John Wiley & Sons, 1993.

Axtell, Roger E. *Do's and Taboos of Body Language around the World.* New York: John Wiley & Sons, 1998.

Beamer, Linda, and Iris Varner. *Intercultural Communication in the Global Workplace.* Toronto: Irwin, 1995.

Brislin, Richard. *Understanding Culture's Influence on Behavior.* New York: Harcourt-Brace, 1993.

Casse, Pierre. *Training for the Multinational Manager.* Society for Intercultural Training and Research. Washington, DC: SIETAR International, 1982.

Dodd, C. H. *Dynamics of Intercultural Communication.* 5th ed. Boston: McGraw-Hill, 1995.

Donaldson, Thomas. "Values in Tension: Ethics Away from Home." *Harvard Business Review* (September-October 1996) 48–62.

Ferraro, Gary P. *The Cultural Dimension of International Business.* Englewood Cliffs, NJ: Prentice Hall, 1997.

Foster, Dean Allen. *Bargaining across Borders: How to Negotiate Business Successfully Anywhere in the World.* New York: McGraw-Hill, 1992.

Haas, Christina, and Jeffrey L. Funk. "'Shared Information': Some Observations of Communication in Technical Settings." *Technical Communication* 36 (1989) 386–387.

Hall, Edward T. *Beyond Culture.* New York: Anchor Books, 1981.

Hofstede, Geert. *Culture's Consequences: International Differences in World-Related Values.* Sage, 1980.

Hofstede, Geert. *Cultures and Organizations: Software of the Mind.* New York: McGraw-Hill, 1997.

Hoft, Nancy L. *International Technical Communication; How to Export Information about High Technology.* New York: John Wiley & Sons, 1995.

Horton, William. *Illustrating Computer Documentation.* New York: John Wiley & Sons, 1991.

Katz, Stephen. "The Ethic of Expediency: Classical Rhetoric, Technology, and the Holocaust." *College English* 54, no. 3 (March 1992) 255–275.

Kostelnick, Charles. "Cultural Adaptation and Information Design: Two Contrasting Views." *IEEE Transactions on Professional Communication* 38 (1995).

Morrison, Terri, Wayne Conaway, and George Borden. *Kiss, Bow, or Shake Hands: How to Do Business in Sixty Countries.* Holbrook, MA: Bob Adams, Inc., 1994.

Randlesome, Collin, William Brierly, Kevin Bruton, Colin Gordon, and Peter King. *Business Cultures in Europe.* Boston: Butterworth-Heinemann, 1990.

Samovar, Larry, and Richard Porter (eds.). *Intercultural Communication: A Reader.* 10th ed. Belmont, CA: Thomson Wadsworth, 2003.

Sartwell, Crispin. "Talking to the Taliban," *Philadelphia Inquirer,* December 4, 1997.

Stewart, Edward C., and Milton J. Bennett. *American Cultural Patterns: A Cross-Cultural Perspective.* Rev. ed. Yarmouth, ME: Intercultural Press, 1991.

Tannen, Deborah. "The Pragmatics of Cross-Cultural Communication." *Applied Linguistics* 5 (1984) 189-195.

Trompenaars, Fons. *Riding the Waves of Culture: Understanding Cultural Diversity in Business.* London: Nicholas Brealey Publishing, 1998.

Tufte, E.R. *Envisioning Information.* Cheshire, CT: Graphics Press, 1990.

Urech, Elizabeth. *Speaking Globally.* Dover, NH: Kogan Page, 1998.

Weiss, Edmond. "'Professional Communication' and the 'Odor of Mendacity': The Persistent Suspicion that Skillful Writing Is Successful Lying." *IEEE Transactions on Professional Communication* (September 1995)169–175.

Appendix 1

Projects for Students of International English

1. Review something you wrote recently. Identify all the words, phrases, and constructions that might be too difficult for E2s. Replace them.
2. Review an article or column from the business section of your newspaper. Identify all the words, phrases, and constructions that might be too difficult for E2s. Replace them.
3. Revise something you wrote recently so that it scores around 10 on the Flesch-Kincaid Readability Index. Now revise it again so that it gets closer to 8. Do you notice any difference in the style? Write a report about the changes, showing all the versions, and comment on the style of the different versions.
4. Review a sales contract or lease you signed recently. Pick an excerpt of 500 to 1,000 words and edit if for an E2 reader. (Do you yourself prefer the revised version?)
5. Examine the packaging and labeling on a commercial product used in the home. Is it suitable for an E2 audience? Prepare a report describing how it should be changed?
6. Visit the two websites you use most frequently. Which is better designed and written for an E2 audience? Prepare a critique, explaining how the less effective site could be changed and why.
7. Review a set of instructions you followed recently in assembling, setting up, or installing a product. Are they in a form suitable for E2 readers? Revise them, using as many lists and tables as appropriate.

8. Consult the policy manual of your school or company. Find two or three paragraphs that are better replaced with decision or logic diagrams. Prepare a report showing the **Before** and **After** versions.

9. Locate someone who translates or interprets English professionally. Conduct an interview to learn what aspects of language are most frustrating and difficult for translators and interpreters; prepare a brief article on that subject.

10. Locate, and experiment with, free translation programs on the Internet. Translate something you wrote into another language, then back into English with the same program. Note the errors and anomalies. Now rewrite your original to make it easier for the program to translate it. What kind of errors did the program make? What changes improved the reliability of the program? Prepare a report.

11. Choose three countries. Learn the preferred letter formats in each country and prepare templates or wizards for use with your word processor.

12. Choose two countries that interest you. Prepare letters for each, in the correct format, in which you break bad news: the end of a relationship or the denial of a request. Summarize the differences between the two letters.

13. Review your own experience—or that of an associate—for instances of well-meaning cultural clashes. How might they have been avoided? Write an account of the incident(s) with recommendations to prevent a recurrence.

14. Choose a country. Prepare a brief guide and checklist for a colleague who is visiting that country on business for the first time.

15. Give two presentations on the same business topic, designed for two different countries. Write a report on the differences between the two and the justification for those differences.

Appendix 2

Sentences that Need Editing

Each of the sentences below contains choices or language that makes it unnecessarily difficult for E2s to understand. Analyze and revise each sentence, using one or more of the tactics described in this text as a justification for your changes.

1. They'll arrive on 6/7/00.
2. Americans tend to understate the downside of their plans.
3. I'm not altogether opposed to a postponement.
4. This is your best and final offer?
5. The new tax law is terrific.
6. They were only hiring two analysts.
7. Next month we'll tackle the distribution problem.
8. What kept you so long?
9. Surely it has not escaped your notice that production is not nearly what was promised.
10. We have empowered our sales agents to be proactive in digging up leads.
11. The footprint of our new desktop is less than 1.5 square meters of area.
12. At this pace, the team will never get to Phase III.
13. The new store will be located a mile north of our current store.
14. Construction will require at least a twenty-month period of time.
15. The auditor raised an objection regarding our depreciation formulae.
16. An increased profit can be realized by offshore subcontracting.
17. The application process will be explained in subsequent messages.

18. To save paper, monthly statements are no longer sent to account holders.

19. This section probably has the most apparent affect on the development of the material.

20. This memo describes our advertising agency selection criteria.

21. Printer assignment is selected from the print menus in the various software used.

22. Analysts make the prediction that lower unemployment rates will impact the Dow.

23. In the new Department, the several security agencies will have to interface more frequently.

24. The Commission reached no decision regarding the responsibility for the intelligence failure.

25. The Style Manual dictates that financial symbols will only appear in the first row of a column.

Appendix 3

Instructional/Technical Passages that Overburden the Reader

Before:

Before using this monitor, please make sure that the following items are included in your package; Kleerview 6SJES/12SJES monitor (1), power cord (1), warranty card (1), "Windows XP Monitor Information Disk" (1), and this operating instruction manual (1).

After:

CONTENTS CHECKLIST

☐ Kleerview 6SJES or 12SJES monitor
☐ Power cord
☐ Warranty card
☐ Windows XP Monitor Information Disk
☐ Operating instruction manual

Before:

From this point the user has two modes of searching. One can choose from one of the sixteen numbered options or do a keyword search. Choosing one of the sixteen options will lead to another screen with additional options. This pattern should be continued until the screen with desired information is visible. A keyword search is also possible from the main options page. Following the same key strokes will once again lead to the main options page, <EQUITY> <GO>.

After:

THERE ARE **TWO** WAYS OF SEARCHING:

1. Select from 16 numbered options:
- Choose one of the sixteen options, which will lead to another screen with additional options.
- Repeat this step until you see the screen with the desired information.

2. Keyword search:
- Follow the same keystrokes to the main options page, <EQUITY> <GO>.

Before:

The accessibility and accuracy of Bloomberg data make it invaluable to the day to day activities in ARG. Any time the veracity of data pulled from other sources is called into question, the next point of order is to check the information against what Bloomberg provides. Bloomberg does not necessarily overrule other sources of data because the data may be calculated or restated in a different manner, but, rather, it is viewed as a red flag and worthy of further investigation.

After:

Presumed Accuracy of *Bloomberg* Information
- Bloomberg data are accessible and correct.
- Therefore, the Bloomberg service is important to ARG.
- Whenever we doubt the truth of other sources, we compare their information with Bloomberg data.
- Although Bloomberg is not *always* correct, still, we investigate any discrepancy.

Before:

At the end of the report processing, the report filenames should display on the screen. If printed directly to the printer, list the printer number and report filename. If printed to disk, list the directory (LST) and report filename. The naming convention should be LST:DELR.lis.

After:

For each report processing, at the end:	
DISPLAY the report filenames on the screen.	
Printed directly to printer?	Printed to disk?
• LIST the printer number. • LIST the report filename.	• LIST the directory. • LIST the report filename.

[Naming Convention: LST:DELR.lis]

Before:

This monitor complies with "VESA DDC," the standards of Plug&Play. If your PC/graphic board complies with DDC, select "Plug&Play Monitor (VESA DDC)" or this monitor's model name (CPD-6SJES/6SJEST or CPD-12SJES/12SJEST) as "Monitor Type" from "Control Panel" on Windows XP. Some PC/graphic boards do not comply with DDC. Even if they comply with DDC, they may have some problems on connecting to this monitor. In this case, select this monitor's model name (CPD-6SJES/6SJEST or CPD-12SJES/12SJEST) as "Monitor Type" on Windows XP.

After:

If the PC/Graphic Card is...	Then You Should...
VESA DDC Compliant	• Open Control Panel • Select the Settings Tab • Click the Change Display Button • Click the Change Button next to Monitor Type • Select CPD-6SJES as Monitor Type
NOT VESA DDC Compliant OR Does not connect through Plug&Play	• Open Control Panel • Select the Settings Tab • Click the Change Display Button • Click the Change Button next to Monitor Type • Select CPD-6SJES as Monitor Type

Appendix 4

A Portfolio of Bad News Letters

The sample letters below illustrate part of the range of styles used in international correspondence. In each case, the objective of the letter is to tell the recipient that a contract for travel services will not be renewed at the end of the current period.

Culture-Free Memo:

In this example, we send a memo-like message, free of justification or explanation, free of sentiment, and free of any of the stylistic manners of business correspondence.

TO: Irene O'Connell
                  Vice President
                  Ireland International Travel, Ltd.

FROM: Edmond H. Weiss
                  President
                  Crown Point Communications

ABOUT: **Ending of Travel Services Contract (CPC0405)**

This is to advise you that **we will not be renewing our travel service agreement** in January, 2005.

The current travel services contract between Ireland International and Crown Point Communications will expire on December 31, 2004. We will no longer be using your services after that date.

If you need any information about the schedule of final payments, please contact David Stone, our business manager at ....

Japan Sample:

In this Japanese illustration, there is an extended, polite opening and great pains to make the bad news seem, if not good, than at least of minor consequence. In high-context communication, dissatisfaction and complaints are better implied than expressed.

August 15, 2004

Mr. Akira Yamoto
Coordinator of Travel Service
Tokyo Business Development Council
15-17 Ginza 9 chome
Chuo-ku Tokyo 104

Dr. Edmond Weiss
President
Crown Point Communications
2000 Cooper Road
Crown Point, New Jersey
03001

Dear Dr. Kobyasha:

Allow us to extend
Our sincere salutations,

Here in New Jersey it is the heart of winter and I remember the poet Houseman's verse: *Fifty winters are not enough to see the cherry hung with snow.*

As the end of the year approaches, we are evaluating our contracts and have decided that, because our travel plans are not likely to include the Far East next year, we shall not renew of travel services contract with your organization.

Your travel services have been superior and we hope sincerely that some day our business interests will enable us to work together again.

Please keep us on your mailing list. We wish the Council great success and look forward to reading about its accomplishments.

Please accept our gratitude for your many kindnesses to our firm,

Australia/New Zealand Sample:

In this exhibit, we use a traditional letter form, but waste no time with buffers or pleasantries. Most students of Australian and New Zealander business communication recommend a direct, factual style, without wasted words or reading time.

November 1, 2005

Arthur Allen
Senior Associate
Western Pacific Travel Consortium
Level 9, 380 Bay Street
Brighton, Victoria 3187
Australia

Dear Mr. Allen:

We regret to inform you that we shall not review our travel services contract with you in 2005. Frankly, we have had too many complaints from our consultants about unacceptable accommodations and inaccurate bills.

We have already made another arrangement, but will be happy to discuss our concerns with you, at your convenience.

Respectfully yours,

Edmond Weiss
President
Crown Point Communications

Mexico Sample:

Mexican correspondence mixes personal and business information. The tone is formal, yet more conversational. The buffer should be sincere, not filled with the stale language of feigned concern.

1 November 2004

Señor Juan Oros
Vice President
Aztec Travel Services
Apartado Postal 99-999
Guadalajara, Jalisco, Mexico

Dear Señor Oros:
Thank you again for hosting our visit at the Aztec Golf Resort. I especially enjoyed dinner with your family and wish your son good luck as he begins his university career.

Unfortunately, the purpose of this letter is to tell you that our management has decided to end our travel services agreement and to book our Mexican and Caribbean travel with our New York agent.

I understand the reason for this decision but will miss our association. Perhaps some day we shall work together again.

Thank you again for your many kindnesses.

Cordially yours,

Crown Point Communications

Edmond Weiss
Training Director

Appendix 5

An Internationalized Website Checklist

Everything that applies to International English Style also applies to English-language websites. And, interestingly, many who consult on the design of web pages in general give their clients the same writing advice offered here to people who wish to communicate with E2. No matter who is reading a web page, the sentences and paragraphs need to be shorter, the access and navigational tools clearer, and the language easier to process and understand. For those who choose to communicate with the world in English, with a single version of their website, here are some now familiar questions that need to be answered:

☐ Which English will you use, American or British?
☐ Does your English web page use only characters and symbols that are supported in widely used character sets in certain countries?
☐ Have you allowed expansion space for the effects of translation?
☐ Does your English text have foreign-language support, such as a utility to translate English words and phrases into other languages?
☐ Have you supplemented your local or 800 telephone number with numbers that work in other countries?
☐ Can people purchase items from your website with a variety of currencies? (Do you list prices in several currencies?)
☐ Are all dates unambiguous?
☐ Are all abbreviations and acronyms explained?
☐ Have you done as much as possible to strip your language of confusing or irritating cultural elements?

❏   Have you done as much as possible to strip your graphics and illustrations of offensive content, value-charged colors and symbols, and other visual distractions?

All these decisions will affect the usability and even the commercial success of your English website. But the truth is that successful international e-business almost always entails translation and localization of your site. Even though this is a book about the use of English as a global language, we must remember that three-fourths of the people on Earth speak no English and that English-only websites disenfranchise all those potential readers/customers, as well as many E2s. Even when people read a bit of English, it is unrealistic to expect them to make purchases on the basis of product descriptions and purchasing terms they just barely understand.

As of this writing, the number of people reading web pages in languages other than English is slightly higher than the number reading in English. By 2010, or so, only a third of the people reading web pages will be reading them in English, and more than a third may be reading Mandarin Chinese instead. So the wisest course for those who plan to do important business this way is to translate and localize.

Today, international e-business planners think of *languages as markets*. Adding a Japanese version of the website means X-million more potential companies. Typically, countries add one language (not one country) at a time, basing their business decisions on the expected return for a given language. Because of such variables as character sets, direction of language (right-to-left, top-to-bottom), and availability of translators, some languages—such as Chinese and Arabic—are considerably more expensive to implement. Again, the decision should reflect the potential increase in market; it should be justifiable in a business case that shows how soon the added costs will pay for themselves.

Translation and localization raise their own questions:

❏   Do we want all our web pages to have the same look and feel throughout the world, or will we make major local adjustments without regard to such constraints as corporate colors?
❏   What translation method will we use; what mix of machines and people?
❏   What portions of our web page will be untranslated (English)?

Have we made sure that these untranslated English words do not
have unintended meanings in the local language? (For example,
gift means *poison* in German.)

☐   Will we support independent websites in several places, or will
the local sites be reached through a centralized, English portal?

☐   Will one need to read English to reach the Spanish or Chinese
page?

☐   Will there be localization *within* languages: European and Mexican Spanish; European and Canadian French; European and Bra-
zilian Portuguese?

☐   Have we replaced all culturally inappropriate images, such as
cars, clothes, foods, and currency symbols?

☐   Does each site have the appropriate number, date, and currency
conventions?

Site designers might also find the following sources useful:

- del Galdo, Elisa, and Jakob Nielsen (eds.). *International User In-
terfaces*. New York: John Wiley & Sons, 1996.
- Fernandes, Tony. *Global Interface Design: A Guide to Designing
International User Interfaces*. Boston: Academic Press, 1995.
- Fowler, Susan L., and Victor R. Stanwick. *The GUI Style Guide*.
Cambridge, MA: Academic Press, 1994.
- Nevins, Madeline M., and Marie Lerch. "Creating and Maintaining
a Quality Multilingual Web Site." *Intercom* (May 1998): 6–10.
- Nielsen, Jakob (ed.). *Designing User Interfaces for International
Users*. New York: Elsevier, 1990.

Whether the choice is to globalize in English or localize in other languages, international marketing is always difficult and error prone. The
website will need several design passes before it works, as well as con-
tinuous monitoring and refinement thereafter.

Index

Edmond Weiss, PhD, is a writer, lecturer, and consultant, specializing in documentation, presentation, and internationalization for business and technical communication. He began his career producing documentaries for the CBS-owned television station in Philadelphia, later managed media research projects for the Franklin Institute, was associate dean of the University of Pennsylvania's Annenberg School of Communications, and recently spent a decade on the faculty of the Fordham University Business School. Currently, he is president of Edmond Weiss Consulting.